Lecture Notes in Computer Science 12920

More information about this subseries at http://www.springer.com/series/8637

Abdelkader Hameurlain ·
A Min Tjoa · Bernd Amann ·
François Goasdoué (Eds.)

Transactions on Large-Scale Data- and Knowledge-Centered Systems XLIX

Special Issue on Data Management – Principles, Technologies and Applications

Springer

Editors-in-Chief
Abdelkader Hameurlain
IRIT, Paul Sabatier University
Toulouse, France

A Min Tjoa
IFS, Technical University of Vienna
Vienna, Austria

Guest Editors
Bernd Amann
LIP 6, Sorbonne University
Paris, France

François Goasdoué
IRISA, Rennes University
Lannion, France

ISSN 0302-9743   ISSN 1611-3349   (electronic)
Lecture Notes in Computer Science
ISSN 1869-1994   ISSN 2510-4942   (electronic)
Transactions on Large-Scale Data- and Knowledge-Centered Systems
ISBN 978-3-662-64147-7   ISBN 978-3-662-64148-4   (eBook)
https://doi.org/10.1007/978-3-662-64148-4

This Springer imprint is published by the registered company Springer-Verlag GmbH, DE
part of Springer Nature
The registered company address is: Heidelberger Platz 3, 14197 Berlin, Germany

Preface

This volume contains a selection of fully revised papers presented at the 36th Conference on Data Management – Principles, Technologies, and Applications (BDA 2020). For this special issue, we have selected four articles covering timely data management research topics on crowdsourcing, data streams, skyline queries, and data protection.

All authors were invited to prepare and submit a journal version of their contributions which have been fully re-reviewed by the editorial board of this special issue. Two papers in this special issue are extended versions of international conference papers published in the DEXA 2020 and ICWS 2020 proceedings.

We would like to take this opportunity to express our sincere thanks to all authors and the editorial board of this special issue for their effort and their valuable contribution in raising the quality of the camera-ready version of the papers.

Finally, we are grateful to the Editors-in-Chief, Abdelkader Hameurlain and A Min Tjoa, for giving us the opportunity to publish this special issue as part of TLDKS journal series.

July 2021

François Goasdoué
Bernd Amann

Organization

Editors-in-Chief

Abdelkader Hameurlain   Paul Sabatier University, IRIT, France
A Min Tjoa   Technical University of Vienna, IFS, Austria

Guest Editors

Bernd Amann   Sorbonne Université, LIP6, France
François Goasdoué   Université de Rennes, IRISA, France

Editorial Board of TLDKS

Editorial Board of Special Issue

Contents

Temporal Aggregation of Spanning Event Stream: An Extended Framework to Handle the Many Stream Models

Aurélie Suzanne[2,3(✉)] [iD], Guillaume Raschia[1,2] [iD], José Martinez[1,2],
Romain Jaouen[1], and Fabien Hervé[1]

[1] Polytech Nantes, Université de Nantes, Nantes, France
[2] Laboratoire des Sciences du Numérique de Nantes (LS2N) UMR CNRS 6004,
Nantes, France
{aurelie.suzanne,guillaume.raschia,jose.martinez}@ls2n.fr
[3] Expandium, 15 Boulevard Marcel Paul, 44800 Saint-Herblain, France

Abstract. The Big Data era requires new processing architectures, among which streaming systems which have become very popular. Those systems are able to summarize infinite data streams with aggregates on the most recent data. However, up to now, only point events have been considered and spanning events, which come with a duration, have been let aside, restricted to the persistent databases world only. In this paper, we propose a unified framework to deal with such stream mechanisms on spanning events. To this end, we formally define a spanning event stream with new stream semantics and events properties, particularly considering how the event is received. We then review and extend usual stream windows to meet the new spanning event requirements. Eventually, we validate the soundness of our new framework with a set of experiments, based on a straightforward implementation, showing that aggregation of spanning event stream is providing as much new insight on the data as effectiveness in several use cases.

Keywords: Data stream · Spanning events · Temporal aggregates · Temporal database · Window query

1 Introduction

Data stream processing has been widely studied in recent years [8,23]. In particular, many industrial systems are now using it to process constantly growing amounts of real-time data [14,24] with applications such as monitoring systems for networks, marketing, transportation, manufacturing or IoT systems. Retrieving useful insights from this continuously produced data has hence become a key issue and a challenging task. A common way to process those non-ending streams is to aggregate events by time windows with respect to the instant they occur or arrive in the system, such that one considers only a restricted but meaningful piece of the initial stream at a time.

© Springer-Verlag GmbH Germany, part of Springer Nature 2021
A. Hameurlain et al. (Eds.): TLDKS XLIX, LNCS 12920, pp. 1–32, 2021.
https://doi.org/10.1007/978-3-662-64148-4_1

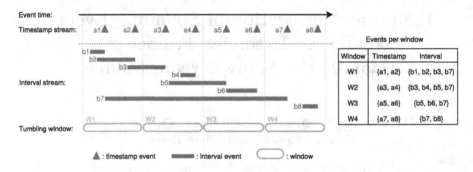

Fig. 1. End time vs. full-time events aggregation in a window-based stream system. $\{a_i\}_{1\leq i\leq 8}$ are point events corresponding to ending times of spanning events $\{b_i\}_{1\leq i\leq 8}$. Event assignment into temporal windows $\{w_j\}_{1\leq j\leq 4}$ is given in the table.

In this popular framework, time is a first-class dimension of streams as it determines how events are aggregated, but up to now, the proposed models and systems focus on instantaneous events. However, there is a need for handling spanning events that cannot be reduced to points in time, such that they consider the entire duration of the event in order to find new data insights. Many applications arise especially in the fields of network monitoring and transportation systems. Let us consider a network monitoring system where we want to evaluate the load of an antenna, with spanning transactions, e.g., phone calls, happening continuously. In a classical streaming system, the load would be based either on the start time or the end time of the event. With a spanning event stream, the full event duration would be interpreted (see Fig. 1).

Using spanning events in this context yields to more accurate results. Figure 1 models a series of calls: events a_i show their reception time, while b_i's show the full-call duration. We want to analyze the load of the antenna every five minutes showed by w_j's. With spanning events, stream intervals b_3 and b_5 span over resp. windows $\{w_1, w_2\}$ and $\{w_2, w_3\}$, while their matching timestamps a_3 and a_5 are uniquely assigned to resp. w_2 and w_3.

Of course, it would be possible to handle both start and end times for each event and then, mimic the spanning event behavior. Yet, natively modeling event duration allows detecting events which have no bounds in the window, like event b_7 crossing window w_2 and w_3 on Fig. 1. Spanning Event Stream (SES) hence allows getting not only information about (dis)connections to/from the antenna, but also to the full connection information, providing from that point more accurate results than Point Event Stream (PES).

SES systems may also receive the events in several signals (e.g., start and end signals), which must then be reassembled to produce the time interval of a spanning event. A streaming system can then account those events from their start, without any need to wait until their completion. In this communication, we will explore different SES models and analyze precisely their impact on the aggregation system.

To be able to provide spanning event stream results, interval comparison predicates, inspired by Allen's algebra, need to be properly set up to allow assignment of spanning events to windows. Furthermore, as a side effect of spanning events, past windows can be impacted by fresh new events without any delay in the stream: on Fig. 1, b_7 not only impacts w_4, but also past windows w_1, w_2, and w_3. Event ordering is also modified by spanning events, for instance the last four events on Fig. 1 can be (b_5, b_6, b_7, b_8) based on end time, but also (b_5, b_4, b_6, b_8) with start time. Those simple observations motivate the need for a close review of the many windows types, e.g., sliding and session, and a new window-based aggregation framework to address SES.

The rest of this paper is organized as follows: Sect. 2 focuses on the formal requirements to elaborate the framework, which are namely intervals, spanning event stream, windows, and aggregation. Section 3 discusses adaptation of common windows to spanning events. Then Sect. 4 details the workflow of a SES system with many options depending on the stream model and the window type. We propose, in Sect. 5, a straightforward implementation of the framework to assess our claim of being an effective model for window queries over spanning event streams. Finally, we review prior works in Sect. 6, before the general conclusion in Sect. 7.

2 Formal Background

In this section, we are mainly introducing building blocks as concepts and notations in order to be able to make a general statement about the problem of aggregate computation in SES.

2.1 About Time

Time Domain. Following the dominant view point, one defines the time domain as an infinite, totally ordered, discrete set $(\mathbb{T}, \prec_\mathbb{T})$. Points (or *instants*) are actually atomic units of continuous time ranges coined *chronons* [3].

Bi-Temporal Model. As in temporal databases [3], one models time with two dimensions: *Valid Time*, being the lifespan of an event in the real world, and *Transaction Time*, as the lifespan of an event in the system. In an append-only system like data streams, transaction time is usually reduced to the start time point, i.e., the instant one records the event in the system.

Time Intervals. Intervals are required at least to represent valid time. As an adjacent series of time points in $\mathbb{T}$, they are entirely defined by their lower and upper bounds, as pairs $(\ell, u) \in \mathbb{T} \times \mathbb{T}$ with $\ell \prec_\mathbb{T} u$. By convention, one always considers the open-closed interval $[\ell, u)$, such that a chronon can be represented by range $[c, c+1)$. We denote by $\mathbb{I} \subset \mathbb{T} \times \mathbb{T}$ the set of time intervals. And for any t in $\mathbb{I}$, $\ell(t) \in t$ and $u(t) \notin t$ are resp. the lower and upper bounds of interval t. Two intervals can be compared with the 13 Allen's predicates [1] which define precisely how the bounds compare to each other.

2.2 Spanning Event Stream

A stream can be seen as a never-ending flow of events where the data is non-persistent and cannot be modified afterwards (append only). In this article we extend the concept to incorporate spanning events with a lifespan as valid time. This slight extension yields to formal and practical consequences that we are about to study. The very first consequence is that it requires to carefully distinguish valid time (range) and transaction time (point) of an event. For this we use a definition inspired from the *physical stream* from [13]. Of course, since data stream applications require near-real-time computation, valid time and transaction time should be ideally connected. It means, for example, that a phone call is recorded in the system immediately/shortly after its end.

Definition 1 ((Logical) Spanning Event Stream). *A Spanning Event Stream* S *is as follows:*

$$S = (e_i)_{i \in \mathbb{N}} \quad with\ e_i = (x, t, \tau) \in \Omega \times \mathbb{I} \times \mathbb{T}$$

where Ω is any set of items, structured or not, that brings the content of each event $e \in S$, t is the valid time range, and τ is the transaction timestamp of e, denoting the time at which the event entered in the system.

Definition 1 generalizes point event streams where events can be represented by a valid time range $[\tau, \tau + 1)$ of one single chronon.

In the following, we denote by $t(e)$ and $\tau(e)$ those time values for an event e. We also use the notations $\ell(e) = \ell(t(e))$ and $u(e) = u(t(e))$ to simplify expressions in the rest of this communication. The notation $S(.)$ is used to denote any projection of the stream S on one or more of its 3 components. For instance, $S(t)$ refers to the sequence of valid time ranges of all the events. Finally, τ_i represents the transaction time of the ith event in S, i.e., $\tau_i = \tau(e_i)$.

The sequence S obeys two "physical" properties:

P1 $\forall e \in S$, $\ell(e) \preceq_{\mathrm{T}} \tau(e)$: an event cannot be recorded before it starts;
P2 $\forall e, e' \in S$, $e < e' \Leftrightarrow \tau(e) \prec_{\mathrm{T}} \tau(e')$: stream ordering strictly maps to the order of the transaction time of events.

A side effect of statement P2 is that, without loss of generality, it disallows simultaneously recorded events.

The above *logical* view of the stream comes from a raw data stream that may encode the events in many different ways. Among the popular options, events could be ready-made, or they could be represented by their start and end time points. We then introduce those two flavors, respectively coined mono-signal and bi-signal stream models.

The Mono-Signal Model. The raw stream provides each logical event at once and carries all the material of Definition 1. As a consequence, an event comes with the full valid time range, and can be received only after it ended. Property P1 becomes P1': $u(e) \preceq_{\mathrm{T}} \tau(e)$.

Definition 2 (Mono-Signal Raw Spanning Event Stream). *The raw representation of a mono-signal SES is as follows:*

$$S = (s_i)_{i \in \mathbb{N}} \quad \text{with } s_i = (x, t, \tau) \in \Omega \times \mathbb{I} \times \mathbb{T}$$

where s_i is a signal that carries all the material of a logical event as stated in Definition 1.

The transformation into the logical stream is then straightforward as it is the identity: $\text{convert}_{\text{mono}}(s_i) = s_i = e_i$.

In this communication, we assume a no-delay stream setting such that P1' is restricted to the equality $u(e) = \tau(e)$. This assumption impacts event ordering, which follows the order of end points of valid times, that is different from the one of the interval set $\mathbb{I}$. For instance, on Fig. 1, b_4 comes before b_5 in the mono-signal stream, whereas it would come after b_5 in the regular interval ordering.

The Bi-Signal Model. Another raw stream option is to separate the logical event into two parts: the first part comes at event start whereas the second part is delivered at the event end. Hence, the first signal carries the start time point $(\ell(e))$ and may partially contain the data (x part) of an event e. As an example, the duration of a phone call or the error messages are not available from the event start. When the data part is missing or partial only, the first signal may at least notify the system of an ongoing event as soon as it starts. The second signal carries the end point of the valid time range as well as the complement of the data part wrt. the first signal delivery.

This model presents the ability to early notify the system of an ongoing event, by registering it as soon as it starts. However, such bi-signal raw stream model also comes with a range of drawbacks: first, it limits throughput since each event occurs twice in the raw stream; second, the mapping to the logical SES is far more complex than the one from mono-signal raw stream. Indeed, mapping in real time the bounds of each current event can be tricky and time consuming: how to deal, for instance, with long-standing events? Or with lost signals (never-ending or non-started events)? Or even with reversed bound arrival order (end, then start timestamps)? Without any additional information, the first signal received would be considered as a start signal, even if it represents an end signal. Thus, dealing with inverse bound arrival and missing events requires to prevent from any confusion between start and end signals. To this end, the raw stream model incorporates an event identifier and a tag to notify a start or end time point. Those extra parameters also allow detecting and handle long-standing events and prevent from memory overflow.

Definition 3 (Bi-Signal Raw Spanning Event Stream). *Bi-signal SES has the following raw representation:*

$$S = (s_i)_{i \in \mathbb{N}} \quad \text{with } s_i = (j, b, x, t, \tau) \in \mathbf{J} \times \{\text{start}, \text{end}\} \times \Omega \times \mathbb{T} \times \mathbb{T}$$

where $\mathbf{J}$ is a set of event identifiers, with j a unique identifier, and $b \in \{\text{start}, \text{end}\}$ is the binary set of signal types. Moreover, $x \in \Omega$ denotes the (piece *of) data, $t \in \mathbb{T}$ is the start or end bound of valid time range, and $\tau \in \mathbb{T}$ is the transaction timestamp.*

In the above definition, the combination (j, b) is required to draw the logical event e from its identifier and the two signals $s_\ell = (j, \mathsf{start}, \cdot, \cdot, \cdot)$ and $s_u = (j, \mathsf{end}, \cdot, \cdot, \cdot)$.

It is worth noticing that there exist two transaction times $\tau(s_\ell)$ and $\tau(s_u)$ for one single logical event.

To transform the bi-signal raw SES into its logical counterpart, the following mapping is performed.

Definition 4 (Bi-Signal Raw SES to Logical SES Mapping).

$$convert_{bi} : S \times S \qquad\qquad\qquad\qquad \to \mathsf{S}$$
$$(j, \mathsf{start}, x_\ell, \ell, \tau_\ell), (j, \mathsf{end}, x_u, u, \tau_u) \quad \mapsto e = (x_\ell \cup x_u, [\ell, u), \tau_\ell)$$

The union operation $x_\ell \cup x_u$ depends on the data.

In the mapping above, the transaction time $\tau(e)$ of the logical event e is the one of s_ℓ, i.e., when the system is notified for the first time about that event. As we assume a no-delay stream setting, P1 is restricted to the equality $\ell(e) = \tau(e)$. Hence, the stream is ordered by start points of valid times, that conforms to the order of the interval set $\mathbb{I}$, but it makes a difference with the mono-signal model (see Definition 2).

2.3 Temporal Windowing

In traditional DBMSs, data are persistent and queries transient. In data stream processing, data are transient and queries persistent! On such systems, queries are continuously re-evaluated as data arrive. Those *continuous queries* face many challenges, among which how to handle blocking operators, i.e., those operators that require to scan all the data set before producing the first answer. Aggregates belong to this class of blocking operators [2,8]. A popular way to bypass this issue is to operate on a bounded sub-stream given by a *window* [21] applied on the entire data stream. Indeed, closing a window unblocks the operation and an answer can be given with respect to the events "inside" the window. Despite the simplicity of the windowing idea, many flavors exist [5,8,23]. Rather than defining a single window, a common practice is to define once an infinite family of windows such like "each hour".

Definition 5 (Temporal Window Family). *A family of temporal windows W is as follows:*

$$W = (w_k)_{k \in \mathbb{N}} \quad with \ w_k \in \mathbb{I}$$

$W \in \mathcal{W}$ is the set of windows families. The W family is similarly ordered by increasing $\ell(w_k)$ or $u(w_k)$ such that there is no window containment. And a temporal window w_k is a regular time interval which delimits a finite portion of the stream that can be assigned to the window query.

We propose in this section a categorization of windows based on a series of measures and generation functions.

Measures. Measures support the definition of the shape and/or frequency of windows in a window family. They could also be combined to define sophisticated window families. To fit the finite window bound requirement in terms of opening and release time each measure is time related. This time can be extracted either from the general time $\mathbb{T}$ or from any part of the stream. Measures are as follows:

- **Stream-independent with a wall-clock time** $\mathbb{T}$: a system clock is used. Opening and/or closing windows are then independent from the stream. Time dimensions used to assign events to windows may vary, among for instance valid time and transaction time [23].
- **Stream-dependent**:
  - **Valid time** $S(t)$ uses the valid time of events, e.g., to define session windows when bounds depend on the traffic flow.
  - **Shape** $S(\tau)$ uses the transaction time of the events; a popular example is the *Count-based* windows where bounds depend on the number of events that occurred until now.
  - **Data** $S(x, \tau)$ uses both the data and transaction time of the events. Most common windows in that category are: *Delta-based* windows relying on a non-decreasing value in the data [8], e.g., a transaction counter; and *Punctuation-based* windows for which window bounds are events of the raw stream, such like a control signal that dictates opening/closing of windows [8].

We denote the comprehensive measure set by $\mathcal{M} = \{\mathbb{T}, S(t), S(\tau), S(x, \tau)\}$.

Window Definition. From that measure set, we propose a couple of functions $(\mathbf{F}, \mathbf{P})$ to define both any window family and the finite sub-streams that can be assigned to it:

- **Bound Function** $\mathbf{F}^n : \mathcal{M}^n \to \mathcal{W}$ is in charge of defining the time ranges, or bounds, of the entire window family. It relies on the previously defined measures and outputs a family of time intervals. Table 1 provides a series of examples of such window families defined from different measures.
- **Insertion Predicate** $\mathbf{P} : \mathbb{I} \times \mathbb{I} \to \mathcal{B}$ is a Boolean predicate that compares two time ranges wrt. a temporal predicate. It is primarily used to decide whether an event can be assigned to a window. The $\mathbf{P}$ function evaluates the events from the stream on the windows of the family given by $\mathbf{F}$. It compares two time intervals, the window range w and the valid time $t(e)$ of the event e, by the way of any Allen-like predicate. For the rest of this paper, we define two specializations:
  - $\mathbf{P}_\triangle$: True if $\ell(w) \leq u(e) < u(w)$, False otherwise. It states that the event stops in the window range and it is suitable to handle point events;
  - $\mathbf{P}_\cap$: True if $u(e) > \ell(w) \wedge \ell(e) < u(w)$, False otherwise. It asserts the event shares at least one chronon with the window.

Table 1. Examples of windows created with $\mathbf{F}^1$ and $\mathbf{F}^2$

$\mathcal{M}$	$\mathcal{W}$	$\mathcal{M}^2$	$\mathcal{W}$
$\mathbb{T}$	15 min each 5 min	$\mathbb{T} \times S(t)$	Session each 10 min
$S(t)$	Session	$\mathbb{T} \times S(\tau)$	5 min each 100 events
$S(\tau)$	100 events each 10 events	$\mathbb{T} \times S(x, \tau)$	50 transactions each 5 min
$S(x, \tau)$	50 transactions each punctuation	$S(t) \times S(\tau)$	100 events each session
		$S(t) \times S(x, \tau)$	Session each punctuation

A Review of Popular Windows. In the literature [8,9,23] some window types are often used, which we will now review and adapt to our formal window definition. It is worth noticing that, within PES, only the event timestamp is required for event assignment to window, and hence for all those window types, $\mathbf{P} = \mathbf{P}_\triangle$.

Sliding Window: Window is defined by ω the range or size of the window, and β the progression step which sets up the delay between two successive windows. With such a definition, several sliding windows may overlap if $\beta < \omega$ or some events could be pending otherwise. When $\beta = 1$, we talk about *pure sliding window*. Most common measures are

- wall-clock time: $\mathbf{F}(\mathbb{T}) = ((i, i+\omega) : i \mod \beta = 0)_{i \in \mathbb{T}}$
- count-based: $\mathbf{F}(S(\tau)) = ((\tau_i, \tau_{i+\omega}) : i \mod \beta = 0)_{i \in \mathbb{N}}$

Tumbling Window: windows form a partitioning such that two successive windows in the family W meet and there is no pairwise overlapping. This property ensures there is one single window at a time and point events can be uniquely assigned to the current window. The only given parameter is the range ω. Tumbling windows can be seen as a specialization of sliding windows where $\beta = \omega$.

Session Window: a session is defined as a period of activity and must be followed by a period of inactivity. Parameter ε gives the inactivity threshold time range. In PES valid and transaction times are equivalent $S(t) = S(\tau)$. Session window family is $\mathbf{F}(S(t)) = ((\tau_i, \tau_j) : i < j \wedge (\tau_i - \tau_{i-1} \geq \varepsilon \vee \tau_i = \tau_0) \wedge \tau_j + \varepsilon \leq \tau_{j+1} \wedge \forall p \in [\![1, j-i]\!], \tau_{i+p} - \tau_{i+p-1} < \varepsilon)_{i,j \in \mathbb{N}}$. It is also possible to define a maximum window size in order to prevent from long-standing windows [23].

2.4 Aggregation

On data streams, aggregates are computed with respect to windows as defined above. Windowing indeed allows us to unblock aggregation operators providing real-time aggregates as Key Performance Indicators (KPI) on slices of the stream S_w. In real-life applications, those user-defined KPIs are implemented as continuous queries that are evaluated each time a window is released.

Definition 6 (Aggregation). *Aggregates $A_{g,W}$ of* S *are the result of any aggregation function g applied on the relevant sub-stream* S_w *w.r.t. the temporal window w:*

$$A_{g,W}(S) = (w \mapsto g \circ S_w)_{w \in W}$$

Standard, let say SQL-oriented, aggregation measures are min, max, sum, avg, and count. As an extension of standard aggregation functions, we may consider grouping, filtering or any other *computable function* on S_w. Sketches or synopses (wavelets, histograms, etc.) are of great interest in this line of research. Of course, each function must be carefully studied and dedicated algorithms have to be designed to allow for real-time computation.

3 Assigning Spanning Events to Temporal Windows

With all the necessary pieces to create aggregation on a SES, we can now detail the modifications that using spanning events implies to the previously defined windows. This impact will strongly depend on the measures used and we will here provide a detailed review of all common windows in a mono-measure context meaning with $\mathbf{F}^1 : \mathcal{M} \to \mathcal{W}$.

3.1 Adaptation of Point Event Windows to Spanning Events

When considering point events, we saw that we can always use $\mathbf{P}_\triangle$ for $\mathbf{P}$. However, this does not apply for spanning events and we have to modify this predicate to take into account intervals. The new predicate we shall use depends directly on the window bounds definition. If the interval was defined with the stream data or shape then we can use only transaction time and keep $\mathbf{P}_\triangle$ even if we are dealing with spanning events. For the rest of windows $\mathbf{P}$ needs to be adapted to use an Allen predicate (see Table 2).

Table 2. Most common spanning event window definition with $(\mathbf{F}, \mathbf{P})$

Window type	Point		Spanning	
	$\mathcal{M}$	$\mathbf{P}$	$\mathcal{M}$	$\mathbf{P}$
Time sliding/tumbling	$\mathbb{T}$	$\mathbf{P}_\triangle$	$\mathbb{T}$	$\mathbf{P}_{\text{Allen}}$
Stream shape sliding/tumbling	$S(\tau)$	$\mathbf{P}_\triangle$	$S(\tau)$	$\mathbf{P}_\triangle$
Stream data sliding/tumbling	$S(x,\tau)$	$\mathbf{P}_\triangle$	$S(x,\tau)$	$\mathbf{P}_\triangle$
Session	$S(t) = S(\tau)$	$\mathbf{P}_\triangle$	$S(t)$	$\mathbf{P}_{\text{Allen}}$

At the end of this short review, we claim that among the most popular windows, stream shape and data sliding/tumbling windows can be used straightforwardly with SES. Time-based sliding/tumbling and session windows must conversely be extended to deal with SES, which we shall do in the next sections.

In those sections we will distinguish between mono-signal and bi-signal stream. Bi-signal stream aggregation comes in two flavors depending on the information needed by the aggregation operators. When all the information needed is present from the event start (e.g., counting the event does not require any additional information), we call this *early aggregation*. When we must wait for the end (e.g., sum of call duration), we call this *late aggregation*.

3.2 Additional Parameters

To deal with SES aggregation windows some additional parameters are needed to account for event duration.

Time-to-Postpone. When dealing with a mono-signal SES where events are released only once ended, lifespan yields two problems: (1) the system should be able to wait for (expected) event completion before closing any window, and (2) long-standing events may be assigned to multiple windows. Figure 1 shows an example of such duration constraint with, for instance, the event b_7 released in window w_4, but assigned to w_1, w_2, and w_3 as well. The main challenge is then to provide in an effective way those windows aggregate with b_7 inside. In a streaming system without any delay, a window aggregate is released as soon as the window is considered as closed (e.g., window upper bound reached). However, these constraints yield to the conclusion that this release date must be postponed in order to accept events that started in, or before the window. We call this waiting time the Time-To-Postpone (TTP).

Definition 7 (Time-To-Postpone). *The Time-To-Postpone (TTP), denoted as δ, delays the window release time. A window w which could be released at τ_w is actually released at $\tau_R = \tau_w + \delta$.*

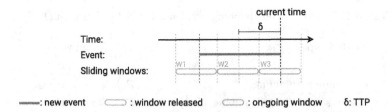

Fig. 2. Impact of the TTP for an event entering in the stream system. The event can only enter in ongoing windows. (Color figure online)

Figure 2 illustrates the behavior of the TTP, where the window W1 has already been released at $u(\text{W1}) + \delta$ since its TTP timeout is over, whereas windows W2 and W3 are still ongoing. The new event (blue line) can thus enter in W2 and W3, but not in W1. The TTP hence as the effect of altering long events, with their start forgotten or ignored by the system.

For bi-signal SES, events are known from their starting point; thus the TTP does not seem to be of use. However, for late aggregation, there is an interest in using a maximum TTP, as we must wait for the end signal of all events present in the window to release it. This maximum TTP would ensure us that windows are released in an acceptable amount of time, and this even if the events they contain are extremely long. Unlike with mono-signal SES, TTP is an optional value in this case. Note that for bi-signal SES eager aggregation, all the information for the aggregation are known from the event start; thus we can release a window as soon as its release time is reached.

Of course, TTP is a patch to overcome limitations of exact aggregate computations for temporal windows on data stream. As a consequence, it can lead to approximate results since events may be ignored and aggregates already released. Adaptive TTP or multi-level TTP are techniques to leverage approximations that deserve to be explored in future works. The TTP value could be defined by the user, with business rules, or it could be learned by the system, for instance from caching policy.

Maximum Event Size (Optional). On the contrary to TTP which is needed in the case of mono-signal SES, maximum event size is an optional parameter needed for implementation. As we just saw, there is a problem for bi-signal SES with a long-standing event which might (1) delay window release, and (2) saturate memory leading to slow down in the system (if not lead to a computer crash). In real life conditions, signals could also be completely lost, leading to events staying indefinitely in the system. To overcome this, the maximum event size prevents infinite events by ensuring that those events are forgotten by the system after a certain amount of time. This time can be chosen as a fixed value with for example the estimated event size and throughput of the system, or it could be attached to a system monitoring tool which would clean up events when the memory is saturated.

Definition 8 (Maximum Event Size). *The Maximum Event Size (Max-Event), denoted as $\mu_{\max}$, represents the maximum amount of time during which an event can be valid and stays in the system. As soon as $\tau_K = l(e) + \mu_{\max}$, the event e is deleted from the system if it is still ongoing.*

The effect of MaxEvent is different for eager and late aggregation bi-signal SES. For eager aggregation, the event is considered, but not in its entirety, meaning that the end of the event might not be included in concerned windows. This is shown in Fig. 3, where the event can enter in windows W1 and W2, but not in window W3 as it has been deleted from the system. This is the inverse behavior from the TTP. For late aggregation, the event is deleted. We miss data from the event to do the aggregation and cannot keep the event longer (see Fig. 3, this time the event cannot enter in any window).

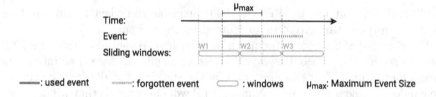

Fig. 3. Impact of the maximum event size for an event present in the stream system. After some time the event is deleted and cannot enter in windows.

Summary. Additional parameters used to deal with SES are shown in Table 3.

Table 3. Additional parameters used for SES depending on the stream and aggregation properties

Stream and Aggregation	TTP	MaxEvent	Effect
Mono-Signal SES	Mandatory	Unneeded	Forgets event start
Bi-Signal SES Eager	Unneeded	Optional	Forgets event end
Bi-Signal SES Late	Optional	Optional	TTP forgets event start/MaxEvent deletes the event

3.3   Time-Based Sliding and Tumbling Windows

Time-based sliding and tumbling window family is time-defined with w and β intervals, respectively the range and step parameters of windows. As a first note, with our SES framework, the unique assignment property does not hold for tumbling windows, as shown in Fig. 1. The focus of this section is to fix the problem of event assignment to time-based windows.

Event assignment to a window depends on how their lifespan compare based on the Allen's algebra [1], an event e is assigned to window w if $\mathbf{P}_{\text{Allen}}(t(e), w)$, with $\mathbf{P}_{\text{Allen}}$ any Allen-like predicate. However, we should take care not to consider *before* and *after* relationships since they require to introduce the negation: "events that are not in the window," and this yields to infinite sub-streams.

For time-based sliding and tumbling windows, window bounds are known beforehand and hence the window can be created at its start bound $\tau_C = \ell(w)$. Released time τ_R on the contrary depends on the stream.

A full overview of the needed changes to deal with SES is presented in Table 4.

Mono-Signal SES. For mono-signal spanning events, release time of the window τ_R depends on the TTP parameter δ, satisfying $\tau_R = u(w) + \delta$.

Bi-Signal SES Eager Aggregation. With eager aggregation, we receive all the needed information for an event with its starting signal. Hence we can release a window as soon as the end bound of the window is reached, meaning that

$\tau_R = u(w)$. This has the effect to allow us to reduce the number of opened windows and thus the release delay and memory cost of keeping windows. When the MaxEvent parameter is used, the insertion predicate should also be modified, to stop using events as soon as they are longer than μ_{max}, meaning that an event can enter in a window if $l(w) - l(e) < \mu_{max}$.

Bi-Signal SES Late Aggregation. With late aggregation, we need to wait for the end signal of the event to release a window. Initially, and without any additional parameter, the release time of a window depends on the upper bound of events in the window, such as $\tau_R = (\max\{u(e)\})_{e \in S_w}$. When considering the maximum TTP δ to limit release latency, the release time is either defined with events in the window or with the maximum TTP, using the one which happens first such as $\tau_R = \min\{(\max\{u(e)\})_{e \in S_w}, u(w) + \delta\}$. When considering the maximum event size, the insertion predicate must again be changed. This time events which are longer that μ_{max} are deleted and are not inserted in any window. An event can enter in a window only if $|t(e)| < \mu_{max}$.

Table 4. Comparison between point and spanning event sliding windows

Sliding	PES	Mono-Signal SES	Bi-Signal SES Eager	Bi-Signal SES Late
Parameters	(ω, β)	$(\omega, \beta, \mathbf{P}_{Allen}, \delta)$	$(\omega, \beta, \mathbf{P}_{Allen}, \mu_{max})$	$(\omega, \beta, \mathbf{P}_{Allen}, \mu_{max}, \delta)$
τ_C	$i \mod \beta = 0, i \in \mathbb{T}$			
w	$(i, i + \omega), i \in \mathbb{T}$			
$\mathbf{P}$	$\mathbf{P}_\triangle(\tau(e), w)$	$\mathbf{P}_{Allen}(t(e), w)$	$\mathbf{P}_{Allen}(t(e), w) \wedge \ell(w) - \ell(e) < \mu_{max}$	$\mathbf{P}_{Allen}(t(e), w) \wedge |t(e)| < \mu_{max}$
τ_R	$u(w)$	$u(w) + \delta$	$u(w)$	$\min(u(w) + \delta, (\max\{u(e)\})_{e \in S_w})$

3.4 Session Windows

Session windows are defined by an alternation of activity and inactivity periods. For this, a minimum inactivity time ε is introduced, and allows to separate between session. Each event received either enters in the current window, or creates a new one when the time elapsed since the last event is larger than ε. An expected property for session windows is that one event should be assigned to only one window. For a safety reason, a maximum session size ω_{max} can be defined to prevent infinite windows. As a side effect, an event could be assigned to multiple windows, breaking the fundamental law of session windows.

Window bounds of sessions directly depend on the events. For this, functions $\mathbf{F}$ and $\mathbf{P}$ use modified versions of event valid time, to account for event size and possible sessions clash due to the TTP. Depending on the type of stream and aggregation, definition of those bounds differs with several possible options. The options which will then be used must then be chosen carefully.

We model the modified event bound as $\Lambda(e) = [\lambda(e), \rho(e))$, where $\lambda : S \to \mathbb{T}$ and $\rho : S \to \mathbb{T}$ are choice functions that make a reference point (respectively lower and upper) for an event. Then the window bounds can be deduced with $(\min\{\lambda(e)\}, \max\{\rho(e)\})_{e \in S_w}$.

The window opening condition is $\nexists i \in \mathbb{N}, \mathbf{P}_\cap(\Lambda(e_i), \varepsilon(w))$, with $\varepsilon(w) = (u(w), u(w) + \varepsilon)$ the inactivity interval of a session.

With PES, one can definitely decide the start of a session window as a fresh new event arrives. Thus, using the chronon interval model, $\lambda(e) = u(e) - 1$, and $\rho(e) = u(e)$, using only the end bound. Event belonging to a window then follows $\mathbf{P}_\triangle(u(e), w)$.

With SES, we must live adjust lower and upper bound, since it requires to define an instant from a set of spanning events. The strategies used depends on the properties of the stream and aggregation. For all SES and aggregation types, event belonging to a window is modeled by $\mathbf{P}_\cap(\Lambda(e), w)$.

Table 5 details the strategies adopted for event insertion into windows: events eligible, upper- and lower-bound functions. Then, the parameters used for each PES and SES session configuration is summarized in Table 6.

Mono-Signal SES. With mono-signal stream, the upper bound of a session depends only on the end of the assigned events $\rho(e) = u(e)$. The definition of the lower bound is more complex as we receive events only at their end and must decide how far back in time we accept to rewrite the bounds of the session. Several strategies can be adopted:

(1) **consider the event as a point event**: this strategy does not consider the lifespan of the event and just uses the event end bound $\lambda(e) = u(e) - 1$ as shown in strategy (1) in Fig. 4.

(2) **consider the full event**: when considering the lifespan of the event, we can first estimate the lower bound as $\lambda(e) = \ell(e)$, such that the event is starting in (and covers) the session. However, this strategy can lead to problems, as illustrated with strategy (2), where the last event is a long-standing event leading to either reopening or creating a session, both of them causing impossible situations since the aggregate has already been released in the first case and the second case leads to session overlaps.

(3) **consider partially the event**: to overcome this problem, we consider that a new session cannot break a past session which has been released. Hence we restrict back propagation of the update, the minimum starting bound of a new session is $l(w) = u(w_{last}) + \varepsilon$ with w_{last} the last session, shown in strategy (3). This strategy makes the long-standing event problem disappear while maximizing the window bounds rewriting. The new start bound function is $\lambda(e) = \max(\ell(e), u(w_{last}) + \varepsilon)$.

(4) **forget the event**: the last strategy is to delete the events which are too long, meaning that their duration is larger than the TTP, $|t(e)| > \delta$. It solves the problem of starting bound rewriting, but leads to even more imprecise aggregation results.

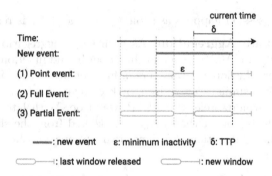

Fig. 4. Three strategies to decide session lower bound with mono-signal stream.

As it allows considering most of the event, without leading to session overlapping problems, partially considering events (strategy (3)) is the best solution for mono-signal SES.

Then, release of the session depends on the minimum inactivity period ε and the TTP value δ, it satisfies $\tau_R = u(w) + \varepsilon + \delta$. Note that several sessions (current session and past sessions not yet released) can be active at the same time, and hence long events can yield to merge two sessions if ε is not observed anymore. More details about session merge follow in Sect. 4.3.

Bi-Signal SES Eager Aggregation. For bi-signal stream eager aggregation the lower bound is defined by the first event we encounter in the window, which is known from its starting time, thus $\lambda(e) = \ell(e)$. Initially the upper-bound function is defined with the event end bound $\rho(e) = u(e)$. When we consider, μ_{max} however, the upper-bound must be changed and three strategies can be adopted:

(1) **consider the event up to its deletion**: consider the event for session bounds even if incomplete. The upper bound depends on the event end if the event is smaller than event maximum size, and else maximum event size is considered $\rho(e) = min(u(e), \ell(e) + \mu_{max})$.
(2) **consider only known bounds of the event**: keep the event but do not use it for upper session bounds until it is complete. The upper bound consider the event only if $|t(e)| < \mu_{max}$, $\rho(e) = u(e)$. This can lead to open several sessions even though there is a long event ongoing.
(3) **forget the event**: in this solution, if the event is longer than the maximum event size, it is completely forgotten. Both bounds consider the event only if $|t(e)| < \mu_{max}$, $\lambda(e) = \ell(e)$ and $\rho(e) = u(e)$. If the event is greater than maximum event size, it does not even enter in the window aggregation results, even though it has an intersection with the window. This leads to a more imprecise aggregation result.

The best strategy is the one who considers the event up to its deletion (strategy (1)). Indeed, it allows to consider even partial events without any risk of breaking them into several sessions and hence provides the most accurate results.

Release of the session happens as soon as $\tau_R = u(w) + \varepsilon$ is reached.

Bi-Signal SES Late Aggregation. As with eager aggregation, initially the lower bound function is $\lambda(e) = \ell(e)$ and the upper bound function is $\rho(e) = u(e)$. When we consider additional parameters, a first remark is that δ is not needed, as $\mu_{\max}$ behaves in a similar way. Indeed, by keeping events for a certain amount of time, it delays window release as TTP would do. With late aggregation, if an event results to be longer than $\mu_{\max}$ it is deleted from the stream, and not considered for the aggregation. We have two options for the bounds session window definition:

(1) **consider event bounds**: the event does not count for the final result but still counts for the session window bounds. The lower bound considers all events $\lambda(e) = \ell(e)$. The upper bound consider the event only if $|t(e)| < \mu_{\max}$, $\rho(e) = u(e)$.
(2) **forget the event**: the event is deleted. Both bounds consider the event only if $|t(e)| < \mu_{\max}$, $\lambda(e) = \ell(e)$ and $\rho(e) = u(e)$.

As long events will not enter in the aggregation result, completely forgetting them is consistent and the strategy (2) will be used. This way, session bounds is in accordance with the events contained in the window.

Release of the session happens as soon as there is no event ongoing for the minimal inactivity time $\tau_R = u(w) + \varepsilon$.

Table 5. Events eligible to enter in session windows and definition of parameters $\lambda(e)$ and $\rho(e)$ for point and spanning event sessions.

Session	PES	Mono-Signal SES	Bi-Signal SES Eager	Bi-Signal SES Late
Events	All	All	All	$|t(e)| \leq \mu_{\max}$
$\lambda(e)$	$u(e) - 1$	$\max(\ell(e), u(w_{last}) + \varepsilon)$	$\ell(e)$	$\ell(e)$
$\rho(e)$	$u(e)$	$u(e)$	$\min(u(e), \ell(e) + \mu_{\max})$	$u(e)$

Table 6. Comparison between point and spanning event session windows. We use $\varepsilon(w) = (u(w), u(w) + \varepsilon)$ as the inactivity interval, and $\Lambda(e) = [\lambda(e), \rho(e))$ as the reconsidered event with the optional TTP and maximum event size.

Session	PES	Mono-Signal SES	Bi-Signal SES Eager	Bi-Signal SES Late
Parameters	$(\varepsilon, \omega_{\max})$	$(\varepsilon, \omega_{\max}, \delta)$	$(\varepsilon, \omega_{\max}, \mu_{\max})$	$(\varepsilon, \omega_{\max}, \mu_{\max})$
τ_C	$\nexists i \in \mathbb{N}, \mathbf{P}_\cap(\Lambda(e_i), \varepsilon(w))$			
w	$(\min\{\lambda(e)\}, \max\{\rho(e)\})_{e \in S_w}$			
$\mathbf{P}$	$\mathbf{P}_\triangle(u(e), w)$	$\mathbf{P}_\cap(\Lambda(e), w)$		
τ_R	$u(w) + \varepsilon$	$u(w) + \varepsilon + \delta$	$u(w) + \varepsilon$	$u(w) + \varepsilon$

4   Processing Spanning Event Stream

The previous section detailed all necessary modifications needed to deal with SES within popular windows. In this section we reuse those modifications to describe the full workflow of our streaming system, from event reception to aggregation release.

4.1   Supporting Structures and Operations

To build a streaming system able to deal with mono-signal and bi-signal SES several managing structures are necessary, to keep windows and events, which will be detailed in this section. Then, common streaming operations to handle windows and event life cycle are required, which purpose will be explained.

Window Manager. The window manager stores for every ongoing window its interval and associated sub-stream, which allows keeping several opened windows at the same time. The definition of the window manager is the following:

$$W_{mgr} = (S_w)_{w \in W}$$

with w a window interval and $S_w \subset S$ the relevant substream. Initially, the window manager is empty $W_{mgr} = \emptyset$. w is increasing with time, following the same ordering as intervals, on $l(w)$. When a window is released, its interval and associated sub-stream are passed on to the aggregation. Once this is done, the window can be safely removed from the window manager.

For both sliding/tumbling and session window the window manager is a FIFO list where the first window created will be the first to be released. Hence checks on the possible release of a window always start with the oldest window and stop as soon as a window does not meet the criteria to be released.

The sub-stream can be kept in two forms, which can both be used by our streaming system (depending only on the aggregation):

- *Tuple based*: events are kept in their original form;
- *Aggregates based*: events are kept in a partially aggregated form. It requires that there will be no removal in the list of events. Eligible aggregation functions are those that allow for splitting the data stream into finite sub-streams, compute sub-aggregates and merge those sub-aggregates. Hence distributive (as *count*) and algebraic (as *average*) functions can be used, while holistic aggregation functions are discarded (as *median*).

Event Manager. For bi-signal stream an additional structure is needed to keep track of ongoing events. This event manager will store start signals only, and is defined as:

$$E_{mgr} = (s_j)_{j \in J}$$

with j an event identifier and s_j a start signal. Once an event is completed thanks to its end signal, then its associated start signal is deleted from $\mathrm{E_{mgr}}$, such that only ongoing events are represented in the structure.

Operations. Processing of spanning events follows a loop, iterating over each chronon. The current time of the system is defined by $\tau \in \mathbb{T}$. There are three fundamental operations to deal with windows in a delayed stream system:

- **Insert** models the addition of a new event to the window manager.
- **Create** defines the creation of a new window and its addition to the window manager. Note that the newly created window bounds might not be definitive (e.g., session windows).
- **Release (or trigger)** represents the moment where the window interval and sub-stream are fed to the aggregation operator. This allows returning a window aggregate to the user.
- **Purge** cleans up the ongoing event list of the event manager. This operation is needed only for bi-signal stream and is triggered just after **insert**.

Those operations are performed at each chronon in varying order depending on the window and aggregation type. In the case of non-delayed PES, the window manager can only keep one window sub-stream, which is the current window [8]. In such a model, **create** operation would be unnecessary, and a new operation, **evict**, would appear to delete events which are too old. With SES, such an implementation is not possible as event entry and expiry times follow different orders, such that each window requires one bucket.

4.2 Time-Based Sliding and Tumbling Windows

For time-based sliding and tumbling windows the operation order is not important. Note that this order is similar to the one for PES [8].

Mono-Signal SES. For mono-signal stream the full workflow is shown in Algorithm 1. As raw signal s is equivalent to event e we consider here that we directly receive the event. Details of the operations are explained below:

1. **Insert**: fill all ongoing windows from $\mathrm{W_{mgr}}$ with incoming event e. For an event to enter S_w it must satisfy $\mathbf{P}_{\mathrm{Allen}}(t(e), w), w \in \mathrm{W_{mgr}}$. With the predicate $\mathbf{P}_\cap$ an optimization can be made to read less window. It starts with the most recent window and stops as soon as the intersect predicate returns false as not further windows will contain the event.
2. **Create**: if $\tau \bmod \beta = 0$, create a window $w = [\tau, \tau + \omega)$ with $\mathsf{S}_w = \emptyset$ and add it to $\mathrm{W_{mgr}}$.
3. **Release**: if $\exists w \in \mathrm{W_{mgr}}, \tau \geq u(w) + \delta$, release the window w.

Bi-Signal SES Eager Aggregation. With bi-signal stream eager aggregation, the sub-stream S_w contains events which can be ongoing or not, as all needed information for aggregation of events is known from the start. The full workflow for bi-signal stream is shown in Algorithm 2, while the insert part for eager aggregation is detailed in Algorithm 3. The detailed operations are the following:

1. **Insert**: identify if the received signal s is a start or end:
   - **start signal** $b(s) = $ start: add the signal to the list of ongoing events E_{mgr}. Then transform the signal to an event $e = (x(s), [t(s), t(s)+1), \tau(s))$, and add it to the generic list of events S_w of all opened windows.
   - **end signal** $b(s) = $ end $\wedge$ $j(s) \in E_{mgr}$: delete the signal associated to its identifier $j(s)$ from the list of ongoing events E_{mgr}.
   - **end signal with start lost** $b(s) = $ end $\wedge$ $j(s) \notin E_{mgr}$: do nothing.
2. **Purge**: remove all signals which are too old from the list of ongoing events, corresponding to the criterium $(\tau > t(s) + \mu_{max})_{s \in E_{mgr}}$.
3. **Create**: if τ mod $\beta = 0$, create a window $w = [\tau, \tau + \omega)$ and add it to W_{mgr}. Directly add to this window sub-stream all ongoing events from the list E_{mgr}, such as $S_w = ((x(s), [t(s), t(s)+1), \tau(s)))_{s \in E_{mgr}}$.
4. **Release**: if $\exists w \in W_{mgr}, \tau \geq u(w)$, release the window w.

Bi-Signal SES Late Aggregation. When all information needed for the aggregation is contained in the end bound, the ongoing list could be modified to $E_{mgr} = (t_j)_{j \in \mathbb{J}}$ with $t_j = t(s_j)$. Only the timestamp of the event is relevant as the information needed for the aggregation will be received with the end signal. This time, the sub-stream S_w contains only completed events, as the aggregation operator cannot process partial events. **Insertion** must be performed first to allow receiving end signals and thus releasing windows as early as possible. The full workflow for bi-signal stream is shown in Algorithm 2, while the insert part for late aggregation is detailed in Algorithm 4. Operations are the following:

1. **Insert**: identify if the signal is a start or end:
   - **start signal** $b(s) = $ start: add the signal to E_{mgr}.
   - **end signal** $b(s) = $ end $\wedge$ $j(s) \in E_{mgr}$: search the start signal s_l such as $j(s) = j(s_l)$ in the list of ongoing events E_{mgr}. The event is reassembled with start and end signal as $e = (x(s_l) \cup x(s), [t(s_l), t(s)), \tau(s_l))$. Then for all ongoing windows where $\mathbf{P}_{Allen}(t(e), w), w \in W_{mgr}$, e is added to S_w. s_l is deleted from E_{mgr}.
   - **end signal with start lost** $b(s) = $ end $\wedge$ $j(s) \notin E_{mgr}$: do nothing, the event is lost.
2. **Purge**: remove all signals where $(\tau > t(s) + \mu_{max})_{s \in E_{mgr}}$.
3. **Create**: if τ mod $\beta = 0$, create a window $w = [\tau, \tau + \omega)$ with $S_w = \emptyset$ and add it to W_{mgr}.
4. **Release**: it can happen in two cases:
   - the oldest signal from E_{mgr} starts after a window end bounds from W_{mgr}, $\exists w \in W_{mgr}, (min\{t(s)\})_{s \in E_{mgr}} > u(w)$
   - the TTP max has been reached $\exists w \in W_{mgr}, \tau \geq u(w) + \delta$

Algorithm 1: Sliding Window Mono-Signal

input : $S \in \mathcal{S}, \omega \in \mathbb{N}, \beta \in \mathbb{N}, \delta \in \mathbb{N}$
1 $\tau : \mathbb{T} \leftarrow 0_{\mathbb{T}}$
2 $W_{\mathrm{mgr}} : \mathrm{List}\langle(\mathbb{I},\mathrm{List}\langle S_w\rangle)\rangle \leftarrow ()$
3 **while** *True* **do**
4   **if** $e \leftarrow read\_stream(S, \tau)$ **then**
5        $\mathtt{insert}(W_{\mathrm{mgr}}, e)$
6   **if** $\tau \bmod \beta = 0$ **then**
7        $\mathtt{create}(W_{\mathrm{mgr}}, [\tau, \tau + \omega))$
8   **if** $\tau = \tau_R(W_{\mathrm{mgr}}, \delta)$ **then**
9        $\mathtt{release}(W_{\mathrm{mgr}})$
10   $\tau \leftarrow \tau + 1$

Algorithm 2: Sliding Window Bi-Signal

input : $S \in \mathcal{S}, \omega \in \mathbb{N}, \beta \in$
      $\mathbb{N}, \mu_{\max} \in \mathbb{N}, \delta \in \mathbb{N}$
1 $\tau : \mathbb{T} \leftarrow 0_{\mathbb{T}}$
2 $W_{\mathrm{mgr}} : \mathrm{List}\langle(\mathbb{I},\mathrm{List}\langle S_w\rangle)\rangle \leftarrow ()$
3 $E_{\mathrm{mgr}} : \mathrm{List}\langle(\mathbb{J},S)\rangle \leftarrow ()$
4 **while** *True* **do**
5   **if** $s \leftarrow read\_stream(S, \tau)$ **then**
6        $\mathtt{insert}(W_{\mathrm{mgr}}, E_{\mathrm{mgr}}, s)$
7     $\mathtt{purge}(E_{\mathrm{mgr}}, \tau, \mu_{\max})$
8   **if** $\tau \bmod \beta = 0$ **then**
9        $\mathtt{create}(W_{\mathrm{mgr}}, E_{\mathrm{mgr}}, [\tau, \tau + \omega))$
10   **if** $\tau = \tau_R(W_{\mathrm{mgr}}, E_{\mathrm{mgr}}, \delta)$ **then**
11       $\mathtt{release}(W_{\mathrm{mgr}})$
12   $\tau \leftarrow \tau + 1$

Algorithm 3: Insert Bi-Signal Eager Aggregation

input : $s \in S, W_{\mathrm{mgr}}, E_{\mathrm{mgr}}$
1 **if** $b(s) = $ start **then**
2   add s to E_{mgr}
3     $e : S \leftarrow$
      $(x(s), [t(s), t(s) + 1), \tau(s))$
4     $\mathtt{insert}(W_{\mathrm{mgr}}, e)$
5 **else if** $j(s) \in E_{\mathrm{mgr}}$ **then**
6   **delete** $j(s)$ **from** E_{mgr}

Algorithm 4: Insert Bi-Signal Late Aggregation

input : $s \in S, W_{\mathrm{mgr}}, E_{\mathrm{mgr}}$
1 **if** $b(s) = $ start **then**
2   add s to E_{mgr}
3 **else if** $j(s) \in E_{\mathrm{mgr}}$ **then**
4     $s_l : S \leftarrow$
      $search\_signal(E_{\mathrm{mgr}}, j(s))$
5     $e : S \leftarrow (x(s_l) \cup$
      $x(s), [t(s_l), t(s)), \tau(s_l))$
6     $\mathtt{insert}(W_{\mathrm{mgr}}, e)$
7   **delete** $j(s)$ **from** E_{mgr}

4.3 Session Windows

Session windows on the contrary to sliding windows have bounds which are dependent on events. This implies that order of operation **insert**, **create** and **release** is important. **Create** operation happens simultaneously with the **insert** operation, as bounds will be created on the fly when events arrive. **Release** operation happens after the two others, as event reception could delay window release.

Mono-Signal SES. In this section we use u_{last} which states the last session upper bound, initially $u_{last} = 0_{\mathbb{T}}$. Algorithm 5 shows the main session operation, while the detailed operations are explained below:

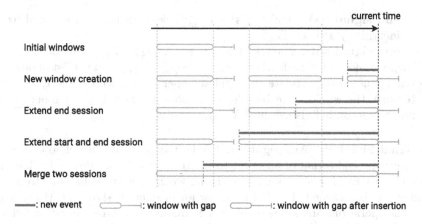

Fig. 5. Different insertion options for a new event in session depending on event size (here we consider the TTP as bigger than all events presented).

1. **Insert — Create**: when an event e arrives it enters in either a current window, or creates a new one. The different session creation and extension cases are shown in Fig. 5
   - $\nexists w \in W_{\mathrm{mgr}}, \mathbf{P}_\cap(t(e), \epsilon(w))$: event creates a brand new session, such as $w = [\max(\ell(e), u_{last}), u(e))$, $S_w = \{e\}$, and add it to W_{mgr}.
   - $\exists w \in W_{\mathrm{mgr}}, \mathbf{P}_\cap(t(e), \epsilon(w))$: the event enters in S_w. Window bounds are re-evaluated, with $w = [\min(\ell(w), \max(\ell(e), u_{last})), u(e))$. When the starting bound is impacted the system checks if a merge between sessions must happen (as shown in Fig. 5). For all windows $w_i \in W_{\mathrm{mgr}}$ where the new session bounds lead to an overlap in bounds $\mathbf{P}_\cap(w_i, w)$ or the inability to respect the inactivity size $u(w_i) + \varepsilon > \ell(w)$, the session w_i is merged with w into one unique session.
2. **Release**: the oldest window can be released as soon as the session is finished $\tau > u(w) + \varepsilon + \delta$. The last session end is updated such as $u_{last} = u(w) + \varepsilon$.

Bi-Signal SES Eager Aggregation. With eager aggregation there is only one window opened at the same time. The full workflow for bi-signal is explained in Algorithm 6 while the operations are detailed below. The **insert — create** operation follows a similar workflow as Algorithm 3.

1. **Insert — Create**: identify if the signal is a start or end:
   - **start signal** $b(s) = $ start: add the signal to E_{mgr}. Check if a session is currently opened:
     - $\nexists w \in W_{\mathrm{mgr}}, \mathbf{P}_\cap([t(s), t(s) + 1), \varepsilon(w))$: event creates a new session $w = [t(s), t(s) + 1)$, $S_w = \{(x(s), [t(s), t(s) + 1), \tau(s))\}$, and add it to W_{mgr}.
     - $\exists w \in W_{\mathrm{mgr}}, \mathbf{P}_\cap([t(s), t(s) + 1), \varepsilon(w))$: event enters in S_w.

- **end signal** $b(s) = \text{end} \wedge j(s) \in \text{E}_{\text{mgr}}$: delete the signal associated to its identifier $j(s)$ from E_{mgr}.
- **end signal with start lost** $b(s) = \text{end} \wedge j(s) \notin \text{E}_{\text{mgr}}$: do nothing.
2. **Purge**: remove all signals where $(\tau > t(s) + \mu_{\max})_{s \in \text{E}_{\text{mgr}}}$. If the list of ongoing events is not empty update the window upper bound $u(w) = \tau + 1$.
3. **Release**: the window can be released as soon as there is no ongoing events and the session is finished $\exists w \in \text{W}_{\text{mgr}}, \tau > u(w) + \varepsilon \wedge \text{E}_{\text{mgr}} = \emptyset$.

Bi-Signal SES Late Aggregation. For late aggregation, we choose to wait to receive the end signal of an event to insert it into the window. This has the advantage to avoid session bounds rewriting when an event is lost due to maximum event size reached. The full workflow for bi-signal is shown in Algorithm 6 while the operations are detailed below. The **insert — create** operation follows a similar workflow as Algorithm 4.

1. **Insert — Create**: identify if the signal is a start or end:
    - **start signal**: $b(s) = \text{start}$: add the signal to E_{mgr}.
    - **end signal**: $b(s) = \text{end} \wedge j(s) \in \text{E}_{\text{mgr}}$: search the start signal s_l with $j(s) = j(s_l)$ in E_{mgr}. Reconstruct event e with start and end signal $e = (x(s_l) \cup x(s), [t(s_l), t(s)), \tau(s_l))$. Delete s_l from E_{mgr}. Check if a session is currently opened:
        - $\nexists w \in \text{W}_{\text{mgr}}, \mathbf{P}_{\cap}(t(e), \varepsilon(w))$: event creates a new session $w = t(e)$ with $\text{S}_w = \{e\}$, and add it to W_{mgr}.
        - $\exists w \in \text{W}_{\text{mgr}}, \mathbf{P}_{\cap}(t(e), \varepsilon(w))$: event enters in S_w, the current window bounds is re-evaluated $w = [min(\ell(w), \ell(e)), u(e))$.
    - **end signal with start lost**: $b(s) = \text{end} \wedge j(s) \notin \text{E}_{\text{mgr}}$: do nothing, the event is lost.
2. **Purge**: remove all signals where $(\tau > t(s) + \mu_{\max})_{s \in \text{E}_{\text{mgr}}}$.
3. **Release**: the window can be released as soon as $\exists w \in \text{W}_{\text{mgr}}, \tau > u(w) + \varepsilon \wedge \text{E}_{\text{mgr}} = \emptyset$.

Algorithm 5: Session Window Mono-Signal	**Algorithm 6:** Session Window Bi-Signal
input : $S \in \mathcal{S}, \varepsilon \in \mathbb{N}, \delta \in \mathbb{N}$	**input** : $S \in \mathcal{S}, \varepsilon \in \mathbb{N}, \mu_{\max} \in \mathbb{N}$
1 $\tau : \mathbb{T} \leftarrow 0_{\mathbb{T}}$	1 $\tau : \mathbb{T} \leftarrow 0_{\mathbb{T}}$
2 $\text{W}_{\text{mgr}} : \text{List}\langle(\mathbb{I}, \text{List}\langle \text{S}_w \rangle)\rangle \leftarrow ()$	2 $\text{W}_{\text{mgr}} : \text{List}\langle(\mathbb{I}, \text{List}\langle \text{S}_w \rangle)\rangle \leftarrow ()$
3 $u_{last} : \mathbb{T} \leftarrow 0_{\mathbb{T}}$	3 $\text{E}_{\text{mgr}} : \text{List}\langle(\mathbb{J}, \text{S})\rangle \leftarrow ()$
4 **while** *True* **do**	4 **while** *True* **do**
5 **if** $e \leftarrow \textit{read\_stream}(S, \tau)$ **then**	5 **if** $s \leftarrow \textit{read\_stream}(S, \tau)$ **then**
6 $\text{insert}(\text{W}_{\text{mgr}}, e, \varepsilon, u_{last})$	6 $\text{insert}(\text{W}_{\text{mgr}}, \text{E}_{\text{mgr}}, s, \varepsilon)$
7 **if** $\tau = \tau_R(\text{W}_{\text{mgr}}, \delta)$ **then**	7 $\text{purge}(\text{E}_{\text{mgr}}, \tau, \mu_{\max}, \text{W}_{\text{mgr}})$
8 $\text{release}(\text{W}_{\text{mgr}}, u_{last})$	8 **if** $\tau = \tau_R(\text{W}_{\text{mgr}}, \text{E}_{\text{mgr}})$ **then**
9 $\tau \leftarrow \tau + 1$	9 $\text{release}(\text{W}_{\text{mgr}})$
	10 $\tau \leftarrow \tau + 1$

For session windows, when events are considered partially (start lost, event lost or end lost) window bounds might be affected. One could add an indicator on the resulting window to mark that session bounds which have been returned are erroneous. This indicator could be a boolean, or a list containing the events which have been truncated/forgotten. In this way, the final user of the session window aggregates can decide a posteriori the way to interpret incorrect session and potentially correct it. This would for example be useful to merge session when a session has been released in two parts due to the TTP and long event size.

5   Experiments

This series of experiments evaluates a first implementation and shows promising results for window aggregates in SES. All those scenarios have been motivated by industrial requirements, especially in the field of telecommunication.

Experimental Setup. In this series of experiments, data is not received at specific instants based on machine clock, but better "as fast as possible." This allows us to determine directly the fastest throughput the system can achieve and allows sizing studies which are valuable for real-life use cases.

Data Set. We use two kinds of data sets: *Generated data set*, this data set allows fine-grained synthesis of the event stream with configurable parameters: event size, session duration, and inactivity. For each time unit (chronon), an event is created, which can be canceled with session creation. The valid time t follows $u(t) = \tau$, signaling no delay in the stream, with a size given by a normal distribution (μ is given as average event size parameter, $\sigma = 2$). When this computed size cannot be respected (e.g., at the beginning of a session), the event is discarded. The generated set is around 2M events. *SS7 data set*, this second data set replays real-world-like data coming from a telephony network. This data set assembles 1 min of communication with 3.2M events. Each row contains 119 fields from which we extract the start and stop time. The average event size for this data set is 16 s.

Aggregates. Aggregation in all experiments is a multi-measure of three aggregate functions: count, sum, and max.

Setup. All experiments were executed on an 8-core Intel® Xeon® Silver 4110 CPU @ 2.10 GHz with 126 GB of RAM under Linux Debian 10.

Implementation. Implementation is done in modern C++, using a single core. It uses an event-at-a-time execution where no optimization was made, following the workflow explained in Sect. 4 for sliding and session windows. The window manager keeps the events with the tuple buckets method, events are stored in *buckets* for each window and are processed as soon as the window is released. To limit the memory consumption, events are stored in the form of pointers. The event manager differs depending on the aggregation version. Eager aggregation keeps started events in a map associating identifier to start signal pointers, itself kept in a map on starting bounds. The structure is simpler for late aggregation, as a map of starting bounds to identifiers is sufficient.

Metrics. In the following experiments, we will consider two dimensions. First, the error rate will allow us to compare our stream processor implementation (PES or SES) to an oracle. The oracle considers events as spanning and computes its results in a know-all condition instead of a streaming one. The error rate is calculated with the theoretical versus the actual number of events in windows (computed with respectively the oracle and our stream processor). Then the throughput gives the average number of events processed per second.

Protocol. In the following experiments we will first analyze the behavior of spanning events on time-based sliding and tumbling windows, then we will have a look at session windows.

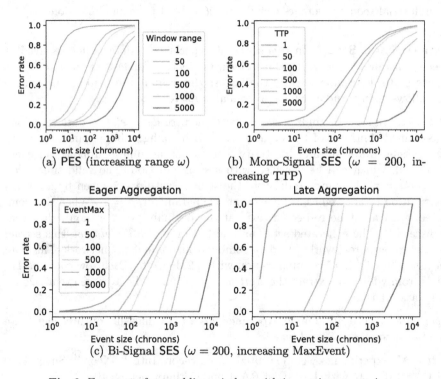

(a) PES (increasing range ω)

(b) Mono-Signal SES ($\omega = 200$, increasing TTP)

(c) Bi-Signal SES ($\omega = 200$, increasing MaxEvent)

Fig. 6. Error rate for tumbling window with increasing event size.

Time-Based Windows. The predicate used for event assignment is $\mathbf{P}_\cap$.

Point Events versus Oracle. As expected the error rate between considering event as point instead of spanning increases with the event size (see Fig. 6a). This error also grows up as the window range decreases. This validates the soundness of using SES to correct erroneous results from PES.

Mono-Signal Spanning Events versus Oracle. When using an Oracle, we can study closely the impact of all the parameters we added to account for event duration. The first one, the TTP, which is necessary for mono-signal SES, must be chosen accordingly to the size of the event. Indeed a higher TTP allows for a smaller error rate, making it compulsory for big events, but small events can be satisfied with a smaller TTP (see Fig. 6b). This validates the need of the TTP to mitigate spanning event issues.

Bi-Signal Spanning Event versus Oracle. The maximum event size is used for both bi-signal SES aggregation types (see Fig. 6c). It has an impact similar to the TTP for eager aggregation, while for late aggregation a small maximum event size could quickly lead to high error rate, as events arriving after this time are deleted from the system. Thus, maximum event size allows for deleting events which are too long, but can lead to bigger mistakes in aggregates for late aggregation compared to a similar TTP.

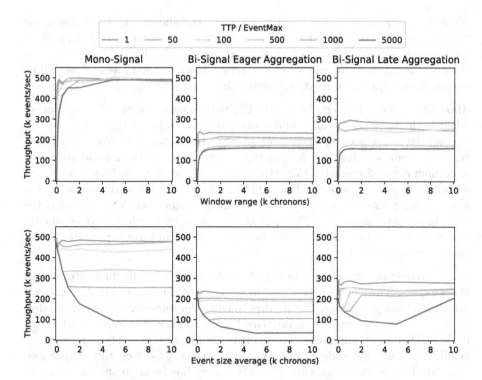

Fig. 7. Impact of window range and average event size (tumbling window $avg(|t(e)|) = 500$ vs. $\omega = 500$, mono-signal uses a TTP, bi-signal uses a maximum event size).

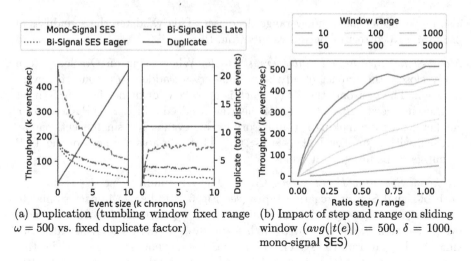

(a) Duplication (tumbling window fixed range $\omega = 500$ vs. fixed duplicate factor)

(b) Impact of step and range on sliding window ($avg(|t(e)|) = 500$, $\delta = 1000$, mono-signal SES)

Fig. 8. Duplication among sliding and tumbling windows.

Time-To-Postpone. For mono-signal SES, when considering the throughput, the TTP has a restricted impact when the window range evolves (see Fig. 7). With increasing event size, this is not the case anymore, as higher TTP leads to consider the event in more windows, and retain more windows at a time. Those extend the computation need, explaining the loss in throughput.

Maximum Event Size. For bi-signal SES, maximum event size has an impact when both the window range and event size evolves (see Fig. 7). This can be explained by the need to keep more events in memory. For evolving window range, we can see that this loss in throughput reaches its minimal when the maximum event size reaches the actual average event size. For late aggregation, with increasing event size, the throughput improves as soon as the average event size has been reached (e.g., when the event is bigger than 5000 chronons the dark blue curve improves). This can be explained by the fact that events are now forgotten by the system. Thus this improvement in throughput also implies an increasing error rate.

Sliding Windows Parameters. As expected, SES yields to many duplicates among the windows. This comes with a cost in throughput: for increasing duplications, the throughput goes down, but it stays roughly the same for increasing window sizes with the same duplication rate (see Fig. 8a). This can be seen for all flavors of SES. This duplication also occurs when the ratio between step and range is small, i.e., near-pure sliding, with the same strong impact on throughput (see Fig. 8b). This is consistent with PES where step has been created as a way to limit continuous re-computations of windows.

Window Release Time. Release time differs a lot depending on the stream and aggregation type (see Fig. 9a). For mono-signal SES, the release time is clearly the TTP. For bi-signal SES with early aggregation, the window can be freed

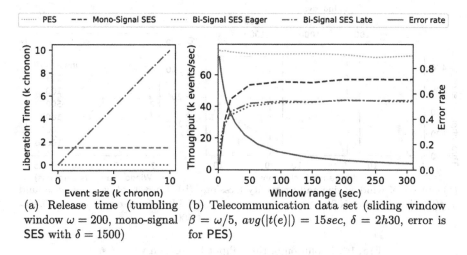

(a) Release time (tumbling window $\omega = 200$, mono-signal SES with $\delta = 1500$)

(b) Telecommunication data set (sliding window $\beta = \omega/5$, $avg(|t(e)|) = 15sec$, $\delta = 2h30$, error is for PES)

Fig. 9. Tumbling window release time and performance on a real data set.

as soon as its upper bound is reached, leading to a liberation time of zero. For bi-signal SES with late aggregation, however, the release time is equivalent to the event size.

Telecommunication Data Set. Requirements from real-world applications are quite high and characterized here by a drop in throughput, which validates the urge to extend our naïve implementation. Nevertheless, on a naïve implementation the throughput of mono-signal SES is only 20% slower than PES, making it able to process around 60K events/second. Bi-Signal SES, have a lower throughput, due to the need to deal with twice more events. They both process the same number of events, with a throughput around 40K events/second. We can note, however, that they make no approximation, as the TTP is not needed and the maximum event size not used in those experiments. Another interesting point deals with the error rate of PES which, as we can see on Fig. 9b, is still around 20% for 1 min windows. Those numbers validate the need for developing a complete SES framework.

Session Windows. Session windows are studied only in the case of the synthetic data set, where inactivity period can be artificially created.

Window Size. As shown on Figs. 10a and 10b, reducing window size as a negative impact on throughput. This is in accordance with time-based windows and refers to how often aggregates should be computed. This behavior can be observed for both mono-signal and bi-signal SES.

Inactivity Period. Figure 10a highlights the impact of inactivity duration on throughput. For both mono-signal and bi-signal SES, inactivity duration has

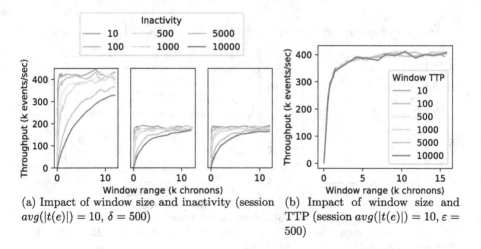

(a) Impact of window size and inactivity (session $avg(|t(e)|) = 10, \delta = 500$)

(b) Impact of window size and TTP (session $avg(|t(e)|) = 10, \varepsilon = 500$)

Fig. 10. Evolution of throughput for session windows.

a negative impact on throughput, although this impact is restricted to small window size for bi-signal SES.

Time-to-Postpone. When maintaining inactivity periods at a same level, we can observe that TTP has no notable influence on the throughput and this for any window size (see Fig. 10b).

Summary. This series of experiments shows that our framework is consistent with all the required assumptions for window-based aggregation on SES. SES is able to correct aggregates by taking into account all the events crossing each window. Then, for mono-signal SES, the TTP allows having correct results, at the cost of a loss in throughput for increasing event size. The maximum event size in bi-signal SES is a metric which should be used carefully as it can lead to completely forget events. While the results of our SES framework are promising, even with real-world data set, it deserves to be pushed further in order to gain efficiency and completely meet the industrial requirements.

6   Related Work

The work done in this paper elaborates on previous work on data stream processing and temporal databases, which tend to be separated fields, even though some links started to emerge.

Window Aggregation in Data Stream Processing. The windowing technique proposed in this paper is a common technique to reduce an infinite stream to finite sub-streams. However a naïve implementation of this approach, like the *bucket* one, does not provide fast enough results, in particular with overlapping windows, where a lot of computations can be shared between windows. Several techniques have been proposed, such as sub-aggregating the input stream [5], and optimizing the aggregate computation with, for instance tree indexes [18, 22, 23]. Studied in the context of PES, we believe that the extension of such methods would be of great interest to fasten window-based aggregation of SES.

However, such techniques are strongly dependent on the window characteristics. A common categorization is given in [5, 23]: *Context Free* are windows which bounds are stream independent, *Forward Context Free* windows depends on the stream but we know their bounds up to the current time, while we do not have such information for *Forward Context Aware*. Each class allows for dedicated optimizations and this should be taken into account for further improvement of our SES framework.

Another optimization comes from the aggregate functions themselves. On this topic we can find some list of available operators in [10, 12, 22] and their properties are a key issue to provide efficient algorithms in our new framework.

Finally, the window approach has been criticized for its inability to take into account delayed or out-of-order streams, and in particular for the confusion between stream progress and stream order [15]. However some methods have been proposed to fix the delay issue, among which an allowed waiting time (TTP in this paper), or the use of punctuation in the stream [12], or even the generation of heartbeats [20]. Another method proposes to maintain a second stream of delayed events only [14].

Temporal Databases. Queries in a temporal database can be of various forms: non-sequenced, where the temporal dimension is not interpreted; current, with only current events; time travel, to look up to a past snapshot; and sequenced, where the query spans over a time range [3].

Sequenced queries are close to our temporal window-based aggregates. However, pure sequenced query is resource demanding and barely evaluated with a one-pass algorithm. Indeed, it often requires to split/coalesce the events time range, which is by itself a key issue [16]. Several methods were proposed to evaluate sequenced queries, mainly with graphs or indexes [6, 11, 17], but as an open issue, only few market databases implement those sequenced queries [4, 7, 19].

Temporal aggregates on spanning events have not been widely studied. In [25], the authors combine windows and full history with a fine-to-coarse grain along the timeline, using SB-tree structure to index events and evaluate the queries. However, the approach is outdated w.r.t. recent advances in window-based stream processing and temporal databases.

7   Conclusion and Future Work

This paper aims at introducing a brand new consideration in stream data with the integration of spanning events. This stream extension yields to redefine common stream properties and usages, such as windowing, and to identify the theoretical and practical requirements to process those events with a lifespan.

In this new framework, we first introduce common ideas to temporal databases with a valid time range and a transaction time point for events in a bi-temporal model. We make different assumptions about the stream order w.r.t. event lifespans such that events are either recorded at once when they have ended, in the mono-signal model, or they are recorded from their beginning in the bi-signal model. We assume that there are no out-of-order events, such that the transaction time point is equal to either the valid time end point in the mono-signal model or to the start point in the bi-signal setting. A future axis of research would be to study the implications of adding delay in the spanning event stream.

The common solution achieved in this paper to overcome the infinite stream problem with blocking operators is to use windowing. To this end, we conducted a careful review that yielded to a new classification of usual measures and the definition of a pattern (function, predicate) for every popular window family and the forthcoming ones. We showed that, among the real-life window families, only time-based sliding/tumbling and session windows need to be adapted to handle spanning events.

Among those changes, we introduced pairwise range comparison, as for Allen's algebra, for event assignment to windows. We also had to define for mono-signal stream a Time-To-Postpone parameter that allows for long-standing events to be properly assigned to past windows. TTP states the aggregation computation latency by postponing the time when a window aggregate can be released. For bi-signal stream, a new optional parameter was added too, to limit the time an ongoing event can stay alive in the system and thus reduce the release time and memory footprint. Introduction of TTP and maximum event size however lead to latency in the window results as well as possible lost or truncated events. For sessions, some choices regarding events retention had to be made to achieve a good trade-off between accuracy and consistency.

In the experiments, we showed that spanning events, represented by one or two signals, can be correctly processed by a stream system: the proposed framework is effective for fixing point event errors when dealing with spanning events. For the bi-signal model, an additional event manager needs to be used, to keep track of on-going events and re-associate start and end signal of events. It has the consequence of slowing down the system, but also impacts the accuracy of aggregation results, in particular for late bi-signal aggregation where an inappropriate maximum event size leads to much worse accuracy than a similar TTP for the mono-signal model. We also pointed out some challenging issues as, for instance, the assignment duplication of events, which is a pain for real-life applications and also, the inactivity range in session windows, being yet another drawback for reaching industrial-like throughput. Obviously, the throughput achieved with spanning events is still lower than the one with points events, but it is mostly compensated by a much higher accuracy of results.

As future work, we anticipate that the implementation should use more advanced techniques in the data stream system to be able to share parts of computations among windows, and hence, compensate event duplication. Besides, delay should be studied in more details since it incurs latency but also make events out-of-order. Finally, extension of the aggregation, such as new operations like grouping or filtering, should also be considered with the ultimate goal of making the system fully operational in real-world conditions.

References

1. Allen, J.F.: Maintaining knowledge about temporal intervals. Commun. ACM **26**(11), 832–843 (1983)
2. Arasu, A., Babu, S., Widom, J.: The CQL continuous query language: semantic foundations and query execution. VLDB J. **15**(2), 121–142 (2006)
3. Böhlen, M.H., Dignös, A., Gamper, J., Jensen, C.S.: Temporal data management – an overview. In: Zimányi, E. (ed.) eBISS 2017. LNBIP, vol. 324, pp. 51–83. Springer, Cham (2018). https://doi.org/10.1007/978-3-319-96655-7_3
4. Böhlen, M.H., Dignös, A., Gamper, J., Jensen, C.S.: Database technology for processing temporal data (invited paper). In: 25th International Symposium on Temporal Representation and Reasoning, TIME 2018 (2018)
5. Carbone, P., Traub, J., Katsifodimos, A., Haridi, S., Markl, V.: Cutty: aggregate sharing for user-defined windows. In: CIKM 2016, pp. 1201–1210. Association for Computing Machinery, New York (2016)
6. Dignös, A., Böhlen, M.H., Gamper, J.: Temporal alignment. In: SIGMOD 2012, pp. 433–444. Association for Computing Machinery, New York (2012)
7. Dignos, A., Glavic, B., Niu, X., Bohlen, M., Gamper, J.: Snapshot semantics for temporal multiset relations. Proc. VLDB Endow. **12**(6), 639–652 (2019)
8. Gedik, B.: Generic windowing support for extensible stream processing systems. Softw. Pract. Exp. **44**(9), 1105–1128 (2014)
9. Hammad, M.A., Aref, W., Franklin, M., Mokbel, M., Elmagarmid, A.K.: Efficient execution of sliding window queries over data streams. Purdue University Department of Computer Sciences Technical Report Number CSD TR (2003)
10. Hirzel, M., Schneider, S., Tangwongsan, K.: Tutorial: sliding-window aggregation algorithms. In: DEBS 2017, pp. 11–14. Association for Computing Machinery, New York (2017)
11. Kaufmann, M., Fischer, P.M., May, N., Ge, C., Goel, A.K., Kossmann, D.: Bi-temporal timeline index: a data structure for processing queries on bi-temporal data. In: ICDE 2015, pp. 471–482. IEEE, New York (2015)
12. Kim, H.G., Kim, M.H.: A review of window query processing for data streams. J. Comput. Sci. Eng. **7**(4), 220–230 (2013)
13. Krämer, J., Seeger, B.: Semantics and implementation of continuous sliding window queries over data streams. ACM Trans. Database Syst. **34**(1) (2009)
14. Krishnamurthy, S., et al.: Continuous analytics over discontinuous streams. In: SIGMOD 2010, pp. 1081–1092. Association for Computing Machinery, New York (2010)
15. Li, J., Tufte, K., Shkapenyuk, V., Papadimos, V., Johnson, T., Maier, D.: Out-of-order processing: a new architecture for high-performance stream systems. Proc. VLDB Endow. **1**(1), 274–288 (2008)
16. Moon, B., Lopez, I.F.V., Immanuel, V.: Efficient algorithms for large-scale temporal aggregation. IEEE Trans. Knowl. Data Eng. **15**(3), 744–759 (2003)
17. Piatov, D., Helmer, S.: Sweeping-based temporal aggregation. In: Gertz, M., et al. (eds.) SSTD 2017. LNCS, vol. 10411, pp. 125–144. Springer, Cham (2017). https://doi.org/10.1007/978-3-319-64367-0_7

18. Shein, A.U., Chrysanthis, P.K., Labrinidis, A.: SlickDeque: high throughput and low latency incremental sliding-window aggregation. In: EDBT 2018, pp. 397–408. OpenProceedings.org, Kostanz, Germany (2018)
19. Snodgrass, R.T.: A Case Study of Temporal Data, pp. 1–21. Teradata Corporation (2010)
20. Srivastava, U., Widom, J.: Flexible time management in data stream systems. In: PODS 2004, pp. 263–274. Association for Computing Machinery, New York (2004)
21. Tangwongsan, K., Hirzel, M., Schneider, S.: Sliding-Window Aggregation Algorithms, pp. 1–6. Springer, Cham (2018)
22. Tangwongsan, K., Hirzel, M., Schneider, S., Wu, K.L.: General incremental sliding-window aggregation. Proc. VLDB Endow. 8(7), 702–713 (2015)
23. Traub, J., et al.: Efficient window aggregation with general stream slicing. In: EDBT 2019, pp. 97–108. OpenProceedings, Kostanz, Germany (2019)
24. Yang, P., Thiagarajan, S., Lin, J.: Robust, scalable, real-time event time series aggregation at Twitter. In: SIGMOD 2018, pp. 595–599. Association for Computing Machinery, New York (2018)
25. Zhang, D., Gunopulos, D., Tsotras, V.J., Seeger, B.: Temporal aggregation over data streams using multiple granularities. In: Advances in Database Technology: EDBT 2002. vol. 2287, pp. 646–663. Springer, Berlin, Heidelberg (2002)

Reducing the Cost of Aggregation
in Crowdsourcing

Rituraj Singh, Loïc Hélouët[(✉)], and Zoltan Miklos

Univ. Rennes/INRIA/CNRS/IRISA, Rennes, France
{rituraj.singh,zotlan.miklos}@irisa.fr,loic.helouet@inria.fr

Abstract. Crowdsourcing is a way to solve problems that need human contribution. Crowdsourcing platforms distribute replicated tasks to workers, pay them for their contribution, and aggregate answers to produce a reliable conclusion. A fundamental problem is to infer a consensual answer from the set of returned results. Another problem is to obtain this answer at a reasonable cost: unlimited budget allows hiring experts or large pools of workers for each task but a limited budget forces to use resources at best. Last, crowdsourcing platforms have to detect and ban malevolent users (also known as "spammers") to achieve good accuracy of their answers.

This paper considers crowdsourcing of simple Boolean tasks. We first define a probabilistic inference technique, that considers difficulty of tasks and expertise of workers when aggregating answers. We then propose CrowdInc, a greedy algorithm that reduces the cost needed to reach a consensual answer. CrowdInc distributes resources dynamically to tasks according to their difficulty. The algorithm solves batches of simple tasks in rounds that estimate workers expertize, tasks difficulty, and synthesizes a plausible aggregated conclusion and a confidence score using Expectation Maximization. The synthesized values are used to decide whether more workers should be hired to increase confidence in synthesized answers. We show on several benchmarks that CrowdInc achieves good accuracy, reduces costs and we compare its performance to existing solutions. We then use the estimation of CrowdInc to detect spammers and study the impact of spammers on costs and accuracy.

1 Introduction

Crowdsourcing is a way to solve tasks that need human contribution. These tasks include image annotation or classification, polling, etc. Employers publish tasks on an Internet platform, and these tasks are realized by workers in exchange for a small incentive [2]. Workers are very heterogeneous: they have different origins, domains of expertise, and expertise levels. Some of the workers might even behave maliciously and try to receive payment without working (they simply return random answers), or return wrong answers on purpose. These workers are often referred to as *spammers*. To deal with this heterogeneity, tasks are usually replicated: each task is assigned to *several workers*. Redundancy is also

© Springer-Verlag GmbH Germany, part of Springer Nature 2021
A. Hameurlain et al. (Eds.): TLDKS XLIX, LNCS 12920, pp. 33–69, 2021.
https://doi.org/10.1007/978-3-662-64148-4_2

essential to collect workers opinion: in this setting, work units are the basic elements of a larger task that can be seen as a poll. One can safely consider that each worker executes his assigned task independently, and hence returns his own belief about the answer. As workers can disagree, the role of a platform is then to build a consensual final answer out of the values returned.

A fundamental problem in crowdsourcing is then to infer a *correct answer* from the set of returned results. Another challenge is to obtain a reliable answer at a *reasonable cost*: unlimited budget allows hiring experts or large pools of workers for each task but a limited budget forces to use resources at best. Last, crowdsourcing platforms have to detect and ban malevolent users to achieve a good accuracy and avoid paying for random guesses or wrong answers of spammers.

A natural way to derive a final answer is **Majority Voting** (MV), i.e. choose as conclusion the most represented answer. A limitation of MV is that all answers have equal weight, regardless of expertise of workers. If a crowd is composed of only few experts, and of a large majority of novices, MV favors answers from novices. However, in some domains, an expert worker may give better answer than a novice and his answer should be given more weight. One can easily replace MV by a weighted vote. However, this raises the question of measuring workers expertise, especially when workers competences are not known a priori.

Crowdsourcing platforms such as Amazon Mechanical Turk (AMT) do not have prior knowledge about the expertise of their workers. A way to obtain initial measure of workers expertise is to use **Golden Questions** [11]. Several tasks with known *ground truth* are used explicitly or hidden to evaluate workers expertise. As already mentioned, a single answer for a particular task is often not sufficient to obtain a reliable answer, and one has to rely on redundancy, i.e. distribute the same task to several workers and aggregate results to build a final answer. Standard *static* approaches on crowdsourcing platforms fix a prior number of k workers per task. Each task is published on the platform and waits for bids by k workers. There is no guideline to set the value for k, but two standard situations where k is fixed are frequently met. The first case is when a client has n tasks to complete with a total budget of B_0 incentive units. Each task can be realized by $k = B_0/n$ workers. The second case is when an initial budget is not known, and the platform fixes an arbitrary redundancy level. In this case, the number of workers allocated to each task is usually between 3 and 10 [7]. It is assumed that the distribution of work is uniform, i.e. that each task is assigned the same number of workers. An obvious drawback of static allocation of workers is that all tasks benefit from the same work power, regardless of their difficulty. Even a simple question where the variance of answers is high calls for sampling of larger size. So, one could expect each task t to be realized by k_t workers, where k_t is a number that guarantee that the likelihood to change the final answer with an answer returned by one additional worker is low. However, without prior knowledge on task's difficulty and on variance in answers, this number k_t cannot be fixed.

This paper proposes a new algorithm called CrowdInc to address the questions of answers aggregation, task allocation, and cost of crowdsourcing. For simplicity, we consider Boolean filtering tasks, i.e. tasks with answers in $\{0, 1\}$, but the setting can be easily extended to tasks with any finite set of answers. These tasks are frequent, for instance to decide whether a particular image belongs or not to a given category of pictures. We consider that each binary task has a *truth label*, i.e. there exists a ground truth for each task. Each worker is asked to answer 0 or 1 to such a task and returns a so-called *observed label*, which may differ from the ground truth. The *difficulty* of a task is a real value in $[0, 1]$. A task with difficulty 0 is a very easy task and a task with difficulty 1 a very complex one. The *expertise* of a worker is modeled in terms of *recall* and *specificity*. **Recall** (also called true positive rate) measures the proportion of correct observed labels given by a worker when the ground truth is 1. On contrary, **specificity** (also called true negative rate) measures the proportion of correct observed labels given by a worker when the ground truth is 0. We propose a generating function to measure the probability of accuracy for each of the truth label (0/1) based on the *observed label, task difficulty, and worker expertise.* We rely on an Expectation Maximization (EM) based algorithm to maximize the probability of accuracy of aggregated final answers for each task and jointly estimate the difficulty of each task as well as expertise of the workers. The algorithm provides a greater weight to expert workers. In addition, if a worker with high *recall* makes a mistake in the *observed label*, then it increases the difficulty of the task (correspondingly for specificity). Along with, if expert workers fail to return a correct answer, then the task is considered difficult. The EM algorithm converges with a very low error rate and at the end returns the task *difficulty*, worker *expertise* and the *final estimated label* for each task based on *observed labels*. Additionally, we propose a dynamic worker allocation algorithm that handles at the same time aggregation of answers, and optimal allocation of a budget to reach a consensus among workers. The algorithm works in two phases. It starts with an initial *Estimation* phase. As we do not have any prior information about the tasks difficulties and workers expertise, we allocate one third of total budget to evaluate these parameters. Based on the answers provided by the human workers for each task, we first derive the difficulty of tasks, final aggregated answers, along with the worker expertise using an EM algorithm. For each task, we estimate the likelihood that the aggregated answer is the ground truth. We terminate tasks which are above the derived threshold at that particular instance. The second phase is an *Exploration* phase. Based on each of the estimated task difficulty, we start to allocate workers for each of the remaining tasks. The process continues until all tasks are terminated or the whole budget is consumed.

A second contribution of the paper is an experimental evaluation of the CrowdInc algorithm. We show on several popular benchmarks that CrowdInc achieves a good accuracy (that is as good or even better than existing approaches), for a reduced cost, and with a reasonable time overhead. This overhead is mainly due to the use of Expectation Maximization, which is an iterative process that converges towards a local optimum. An advantage in using EM is that values of several variables such as workers recall and specificity is computed in addition to synthesis of final aggregated answers. In the last section, we define a simple behavioral model for spammers, and show that the estimation of recall and specificity of workers can be used to detect spammers. We repeat our experimental evaluation, show the effect of spammers on costs and accuracy of answers synthesized by CrowdInc, and show that a simple policy imposing some thresholds on recall and specificity allows to detect most of spammers.

Related Work: Several papers have considered tools such as EM to aggregate answers or allocate tasks. We only highlight a few works that are close to our approach, and refer interested readers to [26] for a more complete survey of the domain. This work compares 17 truth inference algorithms, evaluated on 5 real datasets. The study compares techniques, but also evaluates the effect of qualification tests on aggregation mechanisms. One important conclusion of the survey is that there is no ideal algorithm, and that the most appropriate inference algorithm differs depending on the input data. Another interesting conclusion of the survey is that qualification tests do not necessarily improve accuracy when the performance of an algorithm is already good on a particular dataset.

Zencrowd [4] considers workers competences in terms of accuracy (ratio of correct answers) and aggregates answers using EM. PM [12] considers an optimization scheme based on Lagrange multipliers. Workers accuracy and ground truth are the hidden variables that must be discovered in order to minimize the deviations between workers answers and aggregated conclusions. D&S [3] uses EM to synthesize answers that minimize error rates from a set of patient records. It considers recall and specificity, but not difficulty of tasks. The approach of [10] proposes an algorithm to assign tasks to workers, synthesize answers, and reduce the cost of crowdsourcing. It assumes that all tasks have the same difficulty, and that reliability of a worker is a consistent value in $[0, 1]$ (hence considering accuracy as a representation of competences). CrowdBudget [19] is an approach that divides a budget B among K existing tasks to achieve a low error rate, and then uses MV to aggregate answers. Workers answers follow an unknown Bernoulli distribution. The objective is to affect the most appropriate number of workers to each task in order to reduce the estimation error. Aggregation is done using Bayesian classifiers combination (BCC). The approach in [20] extends BCC with communities and is called CBCC. Each worker is supposed to belong to a particular (unknown) community, and to share characteristics of this community (same recall and specificity). This assumption helps improving accuracy of classification. Expectation maximization is used by [17] to improve supervised learning when the ground truth in unknown. This work considers recall and specificity of workers and proposes a maximum-likelihood estimator that jointly learns a classifier, discovers the best experts, and estimates ground truth. Most of the works cited above consider expertise of workers but do not address tasks difficulty. An exception is GLAD (Generative model of Labels, Abilities, and Difficulties) [24] that proposes to estimate tasks difficulty as well as workers accuracy to aggregate final answers. The authors recall that EM is an iterative process that stops only after converging, but demonstrate that the EM approach needs only a few minutes to tag a database with 1 million images. The authors in [1] consider difficulty and error parameter of the worker. Notice that in most of the works cited above, tasks difficulty is not considered and expertise is modeled in terms of accuracy rather than recall and specificity. Generally the database and Machine Learning communities focus on data aggregation techniques and leave budget optimization apart. Raykar et al. [16] introduce sequential crowdsourced labelling: instead of asking for all the labels in one shot, one decides at each step whether evaluation of a task shall be stopped, and which worker should be hired. The model incorporates a Bayesian model for workers (workers are only characterized by their accuracy), and cost. Then, sequential crowdsourced labelling amounts to exploring a (very large) Markov decision process (states contain all pairs of task/label collected at a given instant) with a greedy strategy.

It is usually admitted [26] that recall and specificity give a finer picture of worker's competence than accuracy. Our work aggregates workers answers using expectation maximization with three parameters: task difficulty, recall and specificity of workers. The CrowdInc algorithm uses this EM aggregation to estimate error and difficulty of tasks. This error allows to compute dynamically a threshold to stop tasks which aggregated answers have reached a reasonable reliability and to allocate more workers to the most difficult tasks, hence saving costs. As the difficulty of tasks is initially unknown, we assign the same rewards to every task realization, and accordingly define the cost of dataset tagging as the number of tagging micro-tasks realized.

Spammer detection has been addressed in several works. We mention below some of works that are related to the spammer detection scheme proposed in this paper, without claiming exhaustiveness. [18] explains that without a priori knowledge on accuracy of workers, one runs the risk of hiring spammers, and even a majority of malevolent workers. The authors define spammers as workers that assign labels randomly without looking at tasks, and propose a Bayesian algorithm called SpEM. SpEM computes a spammer score, iteratively eliminates the spammers and estimates the consensus labels based only on answers of faithful workers. Experiments on simulated and real data show that the proposed approach is better than former approaches in terms of accuracy and number of workers hired. The setting proposed hereafter is simpler: it uses thresholds on recall and specificity to characterize spammers, and does not eliminate spammers during the dataset tagging process. Xu et al. [25] analyze users behaviors during crowdsourcing campaigns. They search for different types of suspicious behaviors to identify spammer accounts. They were able to reveal a complete ecosystem of colluding spammers with this approach. In our work, we consider spammer types that resemble these suspicious spammer behaviors, but we do not consider collusions of workers. Two types of spammers are considered in [9]: bad faith workers and workers with poor competence. While the former are malevolent workers, [9] advocates that the latter are not, and propose to use Machine Learning to detect real spammers based on side information such as the time spent to answer, the number of tasks performed... The proposed classifier showed good detection scores. In this work, we consider more types of spammers. The bad faith workers are called Type 1 spammers, and the second type of spammers of [9] are simply faithful workers with poor accuracy in our setting.

[22] considers a particular type of attack called *sybil attack* where an intruder coordinates corrupted workers to influence agregation answers and earn money. It proposes a technique to evaluate workers reliability using golden tasks, a probabilistic task assignment for golden tasks to hide qualification tests from Sybil attacker, and an online golden task creation from answers of trusted workers to avoid shortage of qualification tests. The framework considered is a static allocation of workers to tasks. EM is used to jointly estimate aggregated labels and workers accuracy. The proposed framework computes a reliability score and a sybil score for workers, that measures if a worker contributed to false answers to golden questions. It assign tasks based on reliability and Sybil score and lowers the weight of workers suspected to be corrupted in aggregation. The spammer detection proposed in this paper assumes independent spammers, and does not use golden questions to qualify workers. Hence, spammers that can only be detected through their unusual accuracy scores.

In [13] an attacker hires a set of malicious workers and can manipulate their label to influence the final labels synthesized, while remaining undetected. The setting proposed is a Dawid-Skene model [3], where the probability to return a particular answer m' when the ground truth is m is given by a confusion matrix. The goal of an attacker is to manipulate labels in an optimal way, for instance by getting high values on the malicious workers' ability parameters to favor their answer. This objective is formalized as a cost function to maximize. The function considers both the success of the attack on final answers and the reliability scores of malicious workers. The optimal value for this function and the associated answering strategy are found with an iterative algorithm. A limitation of the approach is that attackers know the answers returned by normal workers, which is not the case in general. In our setting, we assume that a part of the workers is malicious, but they do not know other workers label, which does not allow fine-tuning of an attack on labels. We hence focus on attackers profiles with simple deterministic behaviors that depend only on ground truth.

The crowdsourcing framework of [8] allows workers to reject a task if they do not feel competent for it, and implements a payment scheme that encourages rejection to favor accurate answers. The framework can contain spammers that answer with random guesses or simply reject every task. Aggregation is a weighted majority voting, and perception of probable reward by rational workers is modeled with prospect theory, using cost functions. Spammers and honest workers exhibit different and distinguishable behaviors. The objective is to find the appropriate weight for every worker in the crowd to obtain accurate aggregated answers and rule out spammers. To encourage honest workers to skip questions, the policy is to pay the minimal reward to workers with poor answers to golden questions. Now, honest workers have a distorted vision of their probability to return a correct answer. In the proposed setting aggregation is majority voting, and the difficulty of tasks is assumed identical for each task. In this framework, the goal is then to assign thresholds for acceptable success rate to encourage skipping tasks, but still allow for detection of spammers and maximization of accuracy of the system. In our setting, we do not consider the possibility to skip questions (i.e. all workers return an answer). We use an aggregation mechanism that accounts for returned answers but estimates tasks difficulty to avoid penalizing honest workers that return wrong answers to difficult questions.

The rest of the paper is organized as follows. In Sect. 2, we introduce our notations, the factors that influence results during aggregation of answers, and the EM algorithm. In Sect. 3, we present a model for workers and our EM-based aggregation technique. We detail the CrowdInc algorithm to optimize the cost of crowdsourcing in Sect. 4. We then give results of experiments with our aggregation technique and with CrowdInc in Sect. 5. Section 6 addresses the problem of spammer detection. It shows the results of an experiment to study the impact of spammers and proposes a simple spam detection technique based on comparison of workers recall and specificity with fixed thresholds. Finally we conclude and give future research directions in Sect. 7.

2 Preliminaries

In the rest of the paper, we will work with variables and probabilities. A *random variable* is a variable whose value depends on random phenomenon. For a given variable x, we denote by $Dom(x)$ its domain (Boolean, integer, real, string,...). For a particular value $v \in Dom(x)$ we denote by $x = v$ the event "x has value v". A probability measure $Pr()$ is a function from a domain to interval $[0, 1]$. We denote by $Pr(x = v)$ the probability that event $x = v$ occurs. In the rest of the paper, we mainly consider Boolean events, i.e. variables with domain $\{0, 1\}$. A probability of the form $Pr(x = v)$ only considers occurrence of a single event. When considering several events, we define the *joint probability* $Pr(x = v, y = v')$ the probability that the two events occur simultaneously. The notation extends to an arbitrary number of variables. If x and y are independent variables, then $Pr(x = v, y = v') = Pr(x = v) \cdot Pr(y = v')$. Last, we will use conditional probabilities of the form $Pr(x = v \mid y = v')$, that defines the probability for an event $x = v$ when it is known that $y = v'$. We recall that, when $P(y = v') > 0$
$Pr(x = v \mid y = v') = \frac{Pr(x=v,y=v')}{Pr(y=v')}$.

2.1 Factors Influencing Efficiency of Crowdsourcing

During task labeling, several factors can influence the efficiency of crowdsourcing, and the accuracy of aggregated answers. The first one is **Task difficulty**. Tasks submitted to a crowdsourcing platform by a client are simple questions, but may nevertheless require some expertise. Even within a single application type, the difficulty for the realization of a particular task may vary from one experiment to another: tagging an image can be pretty simple if the worker only has to decide whether the picture contains an animal or an object, or conversely be very difficult if the Boolean question asks whether a particular insect picture shows an hymenopteran (an order of insects). Similarly, **Expertise of workers** plays a major role in accuracy of aggregated answers. In general, an expert worker performs better on a specialized task than a randomly chosen worker without particular competence in the domain. For example, an entomologist can annotate an insect image more precisely than any random worker.

The technique used for **Amalgamation** also plays a major role. Given a set of answers returned for a task t, one can aggregate the results using *majority voting* (MV), or more interesting, as a weighted average answer where individual answers are weighted by workers expertise. However, it is difficult to get a prior measure of workers expertise and of the difficulty of tasks. Many crowdsourcing platforms use MV and ignore difficulty of tasks and expertise of workers to aggregate answers or assign tasks to workers. We show in Sect. 5 that MV has a low accuracy. In our approach, expertise and difficulty are hidden parameters evaluated from the sets of answers returned. This allows considering new workers with a priori unknown expertise. One can also start with an a priori measure of tasks difficulty and of workers expertise. Workers expertise can be known from former interactions. It is more difficult to have an initial knowledge of tasks difficulties, but one can start with an a priori estimation. However, these measures need to be re-evaluated on the fly when new answers are provided by the crowd. Starting with a priori measures does not change the algorithms proposed hereafter, but may affect the final aggregated results.

In Sect. 3, we propose a technique to estimate the expertise of workers and the difficulty of tasks on the fly. Intuitively, one wants to consider that a task is difficult if even experts fail to provide a correct answer for this task, and consider it as easy if even workers with low competence level answer correctly. Similarly, a worker is competent if he answers correctly to difficult tasks. Notice however that to measure difficulty of tasks and expertise of workers, one needs to have the final answer for each task. Conversely, to precisely estimate the final answer one needs to have the worker expertise and task difficulty. This is a chicken and egg situation, but we show in Sect. 3 how to get plausible values for both using EM.

The next issue to consider is the **cost** of crowdsourcing. Workers receive incentives for their work, but usually clients have limited budgets. Some task may require a lot of answers to reach a consensus, while some may require only a few answers. Therefore, a challenge is to spend efficiently the budget to get the most accurate answers. In Sect. 4, we discuss some of the key factors in budget allocation. Many crowdsourcing platforms do not considers *difficulty*, and allocate the same number of workers to each task. The allocation of many workers to simple tasks is usually not justified and is a waste of budget that would be useful for difficult tasks. Now, tasks difficulty is not a priori known. This advocates for on the fly worker allocation once the difficulty of a task can be estimated. Last, one can stop collecting answers for a task when there is an evidence that enough answers have been collected to reach a consensus on a final answer. An immediate solution is to measure the confidence of final aggregated answer and take as **Stopping Criterion** for a task the fact that this confidence exceeds a chosen threshold. However, this criterion does not works well in practice as clients usually want high thresholds for all their tasks. This may lead to consuming all available budget without reaching an optimal accuracy. Ideally, we would like to have a stopping criterion that balances confidence in the final answers and budget, and optimizes the overall accuracy of answers for all the tasks.

2.2 Expectation Maximization

Expectation Maximization [5] is an iterative technique to obtain maximum likelihood estimation of parameter of a statistical model when some parameters are unobserved and *latent*, i.e. they are not directly observed but rather inferred from observed variables. In some sense, the EM algorithm is a way to find the best fit between data samples and parameters. It has many applications in Machine Learning, data mining and Bayesian statistics.

Let $\mathcal{M}$ be a model which generates a set $\mathcal{X}$ of observed data, a set of missing latent data $\mathcal{Y}$, and a vector of unknown parameters θ, along with a likelihood function $L(\theta \mid \mathcal{X}, \mathcal{Y}) = p(\mathcal{X}, \mathcal{Y} \mid \theta)$. In this paper, observed data $\mathcal{X}$ represents the answers provided by the crowd, $\mathcal{Y}$ depicts the *final answers* which need to be estimated and are hidden, and parameters in θ are the *difficulty* of tasks and the *expertise* of workers. The *maximum likelihood estimate* (MLE) of the unknown parameters is determined by maximizing the marginal likelihood of the observed data. We have $L(\theta \mid \mathcal{X}) = p(\mathcal{X} \mid \theta) = \int p(\mathcal{X}, \mathcal{Y} \mid \theta) d\mathcal{Y}$. The EM algorithm computes iteratively MLE, and proceeds in two steps. At the kth iteration of the algorithm, we let θ^k denote the estimate of parameters θ. At the first iteration of the algorithm, θ^0 is randomly chosen.

E-Step: In the E step, the missing data are estimated given observed data and current estimate of parameters. The E-step computes the expected value of $L(\theta \mid \mathcal{X}, \mathcal{Y})$ given the observed data $\mathcal{X}$ and the current parameter θ^k. We define

$$Q(\theta \mid \theta^k) = \mathbb{E}_{\mathcal{Y} \mid \mathcal{X}, \theta^k}[L(\theta \mid \mathcal{X}, \mathcal{Y})] \tag{1}$$

In the crowdsourcing context, we use the E-Step to compute the probability of occurrence of $\mathcal{Y}$ that is the *final answer* for each task, given the observed data $\mathcal{X}$ and parameters θ^k obtained at k^{th} iteration.

M-Step: The M-step finds parameters θ that maximize the expectation computed in Eq. 1.

$$\theta^{k+1} = \arg\max_{\theta} Q(\theta \mid \theta^k) \tag{2}$$

Here, with respect to estimated probability for *final answers* in $\mathcal{Y}$ from the last E-Step, we maximize the joint log likelihood of the observed data $\mathcal{X}$ (answer provided by the crowd), hidden data $\mathcal{Y}$ (final answers), to estimate the new value of θ^{k+1} i.e. the *difficulty* of tasks and the *expertise* of workers. The E and M steps are repeated until the value of θ^k converges. A more general version of the algorithm is presented in Algorithm 1.

3 The Aggregation Model

We address the problem of evaluation of binary properties of samples in a dataset by aggregation of answers returned by participants in a crowdsourcing

---

Algorithm 1: General EM Algorithm

Data: Observed Data $\mathcal{X}$
Result: Parameter values θ, Hidden data $\mathcal{Y}$
1 Initialize parameters in θ^0 to some random values.
2 **while** $||\theta^k - \theta^{k-1}|| > \epsilon$ **do**
3 $\quad$ Compute the expected possible value of $\mathcal{Y}$, given θ^k and observed data $\mathcal{X}$
4 $\quad$ Use $\mathcal{Y}$ to compute the values of θ that maximize $Q(\theta \mid \theta^k)$.
5 **end**
6 return parameter θ^k, Hidden data $\mathcal{Y}$

---

system. This type of application is frequently met: one can consider for instance a database of n images, for which workers have to decide whether each image is clear or blur, whether a cat appears on the image, etc. The evaluated property is binary, i.e. workers answers can be represented as a label in $\{0,1\}$. From now, we will consider that tasks are elementary work units which objective is to associate a binary label to a particular input object. For each task, an actual ground truth exists, but it is not known by the system. We assume a set of k independent workers, whose role is to realize a task, i.e. return an *observed label* in $\{0,1\}$ according to their perception of a particular sample. We consider a set of tasks $T = \{t_1, \ldots t_n\}$ for which a label must be evaluated. For a task $t_j \in T$ the observed label given by worker $1 \le i \le k$ is denoted by l_{ij}. We let y_j denote the *final label* of a task t_j obtained by aggregating the answers of all workers. $L_j = \bigcup_{i \in 1..k} l_{ij}$ denotes the set of all labels returned by workers for task t_j, L denotes the set of all observed labels, $L = \bigcup_{j \in 1..n} L_j$. The goal is to estimate the ground truth by synthesizing a set of *final labels* $Y = \{y_j, 1 \le j \le n\}$ from the set of *observed labels* $L = \{L_j\}$ for all tasks.

Despite the apparent simplicity of the problem, crowdsourcing binary tagging tasks hides several difficulties, originating from unknown parameters. These parameters are the difficulty of each task, and the expertise of each worker. The difficulty of task t_j is modeled by a parameter $d_j \in (0,1)$. Here value 0 means that the task is very easy, and can be performed successfully by any worker. On the other hand, $d_j = 1$ means that task t_j is very difficult. A standard way to measure expertise is to define workers accuracy as a pair $\xi_i = \{\alpha_i, \beta_i\}$, where α_i is called the *recall* of worker i and β_i the *specificity* of worker i. The **recall** is the probability that worker i annotates an image j with label 1 when the ground truth is 1, i.e. $\alpha_i = Pr(l_{ij} = 1|y_j = 1)$. The **specificity** of worker i is the probability that worker i annotates an image j with 0 when the ground truth is 0, i.e. $\beta_i = Pr(l_{ij} = 0|y_j = 0)$.

In literature,[26] the expertise of workers is often quantified in terms of *accuracy*, i.e. $Pr(l_{ij} = y_j)$. However, if the data samples are unbalanced, i.e. the number of samples with actual ground truth 1 (respectively 0) is much larger than the number of samples with ground truth 0 (respectively 1), defining competences in terms of *accuracy* leads to bias. Indeed, a worker who is good in

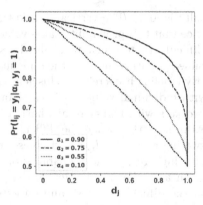

Fig. 1. Generative function for the probability to get $l_{ij} = 1$, given $y_j = 1$, for growing values of task difficulty. The curves represent different recall values for the considered workers.

classifying images with ground truth 1 can obtain bad scores when classifying image with ground truth 0, and yet get a good accuracy (this can be the case of a worker that always answers 1 when choosing a label for a task). *Recall* and *Specificity* overcomes the problem of bias and separates the worker expertise, considering their ability to answer correctly when the ground truth is 0 and when it is 1, and hence give a more precise representation of workers competences.

Recall and specificity allow us to build a probabilistic model (a generative model) for workers answers. We assume that workers have constant behaviors and are faithful, i.e. do not return wrong answers intentionally. We also assume that workers do not collaborate (their answers are independent variables). Under these assumptions, knowing the recall α_i and specificity β_i of a worker i, we build a model that generates the probability that he returns an *observed label* l_{ij} for a task j with difficulty d_j:

$$Pr(l_{ij} = y_j | d_j, \alpha_i, y_j = 1) = \frac{1 + (1 - d_j)^{(1-\alpha_i)}}{2} \tag{3}$$

$$Pr(l_{ij} = y_j | d_j, \beta_i, y_j = 0) = \frac{1 + (1 - d_j)^{(1-\beta_i)}}{2} \tag{4}$$

In the rest of the paper, we use pools of synthetic users with different recalls and specificities following Eqs. 3 and 4. Though experiments with synthetic workers does not replace real field experiments on real platforms, this allowed us to test many variants of the dynamic worker allocation scheme proposed hereafter. The functions of Eqs. 3 and 4 obviously share characteristics of faithful workers: the probability of a correct Boolean answer decreases with the difficulty of tasks and with recall (resp. with specificity), and remains 1/2 even for completely incompetent workers, who cannot do better than a random guess. Figure 1 shows the probability of associating label 1 to a task for which the ground truth is 1 when the difficulty of the tagging task varies, and for different values of recall.

The range of task difficulty is $[0, 1]$. The vertical axis is the probability of getting $l_{ij} = 1$. One can notice that this probability takes values between 0.5 and 1. Indeed, if a task is too difficult, then returning a value is close to making a random guess of a binary value. Unsurprisingly, as the difficulty of a task increases, the probability of correctly labeling it decreases. This generative function applies for every worker, but with individual values for recalls and specificities. For a fixed difficulty of task, workers with higher recalls have a higher probability to correctly label a task. Also, note that when the difficulty of a task approaches 1, the probability of answering with label $l_{ij} = 1$ decreases for every value of α_j. However, for workers with high recall, the probability of a correct annotation is always greater than with a smaller recall. Hence, the probability of correct answer depends both on the difficulty of task and on expertise of the worker realizing the task.

3.1 Aggregating Answers

For a given task j, with unknown difficulty d_j, the answers returned by k workers (observed data) is a set $L_j = \{l_{1j}, \ldots, l_{kj}\}$, where l_{ij} is the answer of worker i to task j. In addition, workers expertise are vectors of parameters $\alpha = \{\alpha_1, \ldots \alpha_k\}$ and $\beta = \{\beta_1, \ldots \beta_k\}$ and are also unknown. The goal is to infer the final label y_j, and to derive the most probable values for d_j, α_i, β_i, given the observed answers of workers. We use a standard EM approach to infer the most probable actual answer $Y = \{y_1, \ldots y_n\}$ along with the hidden parameters $\Theta = \{d_j, \alpha_i, \beta_i\}$. Let us consider the E and M phases of the algorithm.

E Step: We assume that all answers in $L = \bigcup_{1 \leq j \leq k} L_j$ are independently given by the workers as there is no collaboration between them. So, in every $L_j = \{l_{1j}, \ldots, l_{kj}\}$, l_{ij}'s are independently sampled variables. We compute the posterior probability of $y_j \in \{0, 1\}$ for a given task j given the difficulty of task d_j, worker expertise $\alpha_i, \beta_i, i \leq k$ and the worker answers $L_j = \{l_{ij} \mid i \in 1..k\}$. Using Bayes' theorem, considering a particular value $\lambda \in \{0, 1\}$ we have:

$$Pr[y_j = \lambda | L_j, \alpha, \beta, d_j] = \frac{Pr(L_j | y_j = \lambda, \alpha, \beta, d_j) \cdot Pr(y_j = \lambda | \alpha, \beta, d_j)}{Pr(L_j | \alpha, \beta, d_j)} \quad (5)$$

One can remark that y_j and α, β, d_j are independent variables. We assume that both values of y_j are equiprobable, i.e. $Pr(y_j = 0) = Pr(y_j = 1) = \frac{1}{2}$. We hence get:

$$Pr[y_j = \lambda | L_j, \alpha, \beta, d_j] = \frac{Pr(L_j | y_j = \lambda, \alpha, \beta, d_j) \cdot Pr(y_j = \lambda)}{Pr(L_j | \alpha, \beta, d_j)} = \frac{Pr(L_j | y_j = \lambda, \alpha, \beta, d_j) \cdot \frac{1}{2}}{Pr(L_j | \alpha, \beta, d_j)} \quad (6)$$

Similarly, the probability to obtain a particular set of labels is given by:

$$Pr(L_j \mid \alpha, \beta, d_j) = \frac{1}{2} \cdot Pr(L_j \mid y_j = 0, \alpha, \beta, d_j) + \frac{1}{2} \cdot Pr(L_j \mid y_j = 1, \alpha, \beta, d_j) \quad (7)$$

Overall we obtain:

$$Pr[y_j = \lambda | L_j, \alpha, \beta, d_j] = \frac{Pr(L_j | y_j = \lambda, \alpha, \beta, d_j)}{Pr(L_j | y_j = 0, \alpha, \beta, d_j) + Pr(L_j | y_j = 1, \alpha, \beta, d_j)} \quad (8)$$

Let us consider one of these terms, and let us assume that every l_{ij} in L_j takes a value λ_i. We have

$$Pr(L_j \mid y_j = \lambda, \alpha, \beta, d_j) = \prod_{i=1}^{k} Pr(l_{ij} = \lambda_i \mid \alpha_i, \beta_i, d_j, y_j = \lambda) \qquad (9)$$

If $\lambda_i = 0$ then $Pr(l_{ij} = \lambda_i \mid \alpha_i, \beta_i, d_j, y_j = 0)$ is the probability to classify correctly a 0 as 0, as defined in Eq. 4 denoted by $\delta_{ij} = \frac{1+(1-d_j)^{(1-\beta_i)}}{2}$. Similarly, if $\lambda_i = 1$ then $Pr(l_{ij} = \lambda_i \mid \alpha_i, \beta_i, d_j, y_j = 1)$ is the probability to classify correctly a 1 as 1, expressed in Eq. 3 and denoted by $\gamma_{ij} = \frac{1+(1-d_j)^{(1-\alpha_i)}}{2}$. Then the probability to classify $y_j = 1$ as $\lambda_i = 0$ is $(1 - \gamma_{ij})$ and the probability to classify $y_j = 1$ as $\lambda_i = 0$ is $(1 - \delta_{ij})$. We hence have $Pr(l_{ij} = \lambda_i \mid \alpha_i, \beta_i, d_j, y_j = 0) = (1 - \lambda_i) \cdot \delta_{ij} + \lambda_i \cdot (1 - \gamma_{ij})$. Similarly, we can write $Pr(l_{ij} = \lambda_i \mid \alpha_i, \beta_i, d_j, y_j = 1) = \lambda_i \cdot \gamma_{ij} + (1 - \lambda_i) \cdot (1 - \delta_{ij})$. So Eq. 8 rewrites as:

$$
\begin{aligned}
Pr[y_j = \lambda | L_j, \alpha, \beta, d_j] &= \frac{\prod_{i=1}^{k} Pr(l_{ij} = \lambda_i \mid y_j = \lambda, \alpha_i, \beta_i, d_j)}{Pr(L_j \mid y_j = 0, \alpha, \beta, d_j) + Pr(L_j \mid y_j = 1, \alpha, \beta, d_j)} \\
&= \frac{\prod_{i=1}^{k}(1 - \lambda).[(1 - \lambda_i)\delta_{ij} + \lambda_i(1 - \gamma_{ij})] + \lambda.[\lambda_i.\gamma_{ij} + (1 - \lambda_i)(1 - \delta_{ij})]}{Pr(L_j \mid y_j = 0, \alpha, \beta, d_j) + Pr(L_j \mid y_j = 1, \alpha, \beta, d_j)} \\
&= \frac{\prod_{i=1}^{k}(1 - \lambda).[(1 - \lambda_p)\delta_{ij} + \lambda_p(1 - \gamma_{ij})] + \lambda.[\lambda_p.\gamma_{ij} + (1 - \lambda_p)(1 - \delta_{ij})]}{\prod_{i=1}^{k}(1 - \lambda_i)\delta_{ij} + \lambda_i \cdot (1 - \gamma_{ij}) + \prod_{i=1}^{k} \lambda_i.\gamma_{ij} + (1 - \lambda_i)(1 - \delta_{ij})}
\end{aligned}
\qquad (10)
$$

In the E step, as every α_i, β_i, d_j is fixed, one can compute $\mathbb{E}[y_j | L_j, \alpha_i, \beta_i, d_j]$ and also choose as final value for y_j the value $\lambda \in \{0, 1\}$ such that $Pr[y_j = \lambda | L_j, \alpha_i, \beta_i, d_j] > Pr[y_j = (1 - \lambda) | L_j, \alpha_i, \beta_i, d_j]$. We can also estimate the likelihood for the values of variables $P(L \cup Y \mid \theta)$ for parameters $\theta = \{\alpha, \beta, d\}$, as $Pr(y_j = \lambda, L \mid \theta) = Pr(y_j = \lambda, L).Pr(L_j \mid y_j = \lambda, \theta) = Pr(y_j = \lambda).Pr(L_j \mid y_j = \lambda, \theta)$.

M Step: With respect to the estimated posterior probabilities of Y computed during the E phase of the algorithm, we compute the parameters θ that maximize $Q(\theta, \theta^t)$. Let θ^t be the value of parameters computed at step t of the algorithm. We use the observed values of L, and the previous expectation for Y. We maximize $Q'(\theta, \theta^t) = \mathbb{E}[log Pr(L, Y \mid \theta) \mid L, \theta^t]$ (we refer interested readers to [6]-Chap. 9 and [5] for explanations showing why this is equivalent to maximizing $Q(\theta, \theta^t)$). We can hence compute the next value as: $\theta^{t+1} = \arg \max_{\theta} Q'(\theta, \theta^t)$. Here in our context the values of θ are α_i, β_i, d_j. We maximize $Q'(\theta, \theta^t)$ using a bounded optimization techniques, namely the truncated Newton algorithm [14] provided by the standard SciPy[1] implementation. We iterate E and M steps, computing at each iteration t the posterior probability and the parameters θ^t that maximize $Q'(\theta, \theta^t)$. The algorithm converges, and stops when the improvement (difference between two successive joint log-likelihood values) is below a threshold, fixed in our case to $1e^{-7}$.

---

[1] docs.scipy.org/doc/scipy/reference/generated/scipy.optimize.minimize.html.

4   Cost Model

A drawback of many crowdsourcing approaches is that task distribution is static, i.e. tasks are distributed to a fixed number of workers, without considering their difficulty, nor checking if a consensus can be reached with fewer workers. Consider again the simple Boolean tagging setting, but where every task realization is paid, and with a fixed total budget B_0 provided by the client. For simplicity, we assume that all workers receive 1 unit of credit for each realized task. Hence, to solve n Boolean tagging tasks, one can hire only B_0/n workers per task. In this section, we show a worker allocation algorithm that builds on collected answers and estimated difficulty to distribute tasks to worker at runtime, and show its efficiency with respect to other approaches.

Our algorithm works in rounds. At each round, only a subset $T_{avl} \subseteq T$ of the initial tasks remains to be evaluated. We remember labels produced by workers at preceding rounds, and collect new labels produced by new workers hired for this round to realize these tasks. We aggregate answers using the EM approach described in Sect. 3. We denote by y_j^q as the final aggregated answer for task j at round q, d_j^q is the current *difficulty* of task and α_i^q, β_i^q denotes the estimated *expertise* of a worker i at round q. We let $D^q = \{d_1^q \ldots d_j^q\}$ denote the set of all difficulties estimated as round q. We fix a maximal step size $\tau \geq 1$, that is the maximal number of workers that can be hired during a round for a particular task. For every task $t_j \in T_{avl}$ with difficulty d_j^q at round q, we allocate $\mathbf{a}_j^q = \lceil (d_j^q \times \tau)/\max(D^q) \rceil$ workers for the next round. Once all answers for a task have been received, the EM aggregation can compute a final label $y_j^q \in \{0, 1\}$ and difficulty d_j^q for every task t_j, and the expertise of all workers $\alpha_1^q, \ldots, \alpha_k^q, \beta_1^q, \ldots, \beta_k^q$. Now, it remains to decide whether the confidence in answer y_j^q obtained at round q is sufficient (in which case, we do not allocate workers to this task in the next rounds). Let k_j^q be the number of answers obtained for task j at round q. The *confidence* $\hat{c}_j^q$ in a final label y_j^q is defined as follows:

$$\hat{c}_j^q(y_j^q = 1) = \frac{1}{k_j^q} \cdot \sum_{i=1}^{k_j^q} \left\{ l_{ij} \times \left(\frac{1 + (1 - d_j^q)^{(1 - \alpha_i^q)}}{2} \right) + (1 - l_{ij}) \times \left(1 - \frac{1 + (1 - d_j^q)^{(1 - \alpha_i^q)}}{2} \right) \right\} \quad (11)$$

$$\hat{c}_j^q(y_j^q = 0) = \frac{1}{k_j^q} \cdot \sum_{i=1}^{k_j^q} \left\{ (1 - l_{ij}) \times \left(\frac{1 + (1 - d_j^q)^{(1 - \beta_i^q)}}{2} \right) + (l_{ij}) \times \left(1 - \frac{1 + (1 - d_j^q)^{(1 - \beta_i^q)}}{2} \right) \right\} \quad (12)$$

Intuitively, each worker adds its probability of doing an error, which depends on the final label y_j^q estimated at round q and on his competences, i.e. on the probability to choose $l_{ij} = y_j^q$. Let us now show when to stop the rounds of our evaluation algorithm. We start with n tasks, and let T_{avl} denote the set of remaining tasks at round q. We define $r^q \in [0, 1]$ as the ratio of task that are still considered at round q compared to the initial number of task, i.e. $r^q = \frac{|T_{avl}|}{n}$. We start with an initial budget B_0, and denote by B_c^q the total budget consumed at round q. We denote by $\mathcal{B}^q$ the fraction of budget consumed at that current instance, $\mathcal{B}^q = \frac{B_c^q}{B_0}$. We define the stopping threshold $Th^q \in [0.5, 1.0]$ as $Th^q = \frac{1 + (1 - \mathcal{B}^q)^{r^q}}{2}$.

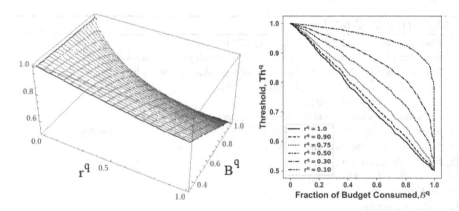

Fig. 2. Evolution of threshold for fixed fraction of consumed budget and fraction of task remaining at the beginning of a round.

The intuition behind this function is simple: when the number of remaining tasks decreases, one can afford a higher confidence threshold, because the maximal budget needed to solve all tasks decreases too. Similarly, as the budget decreases, one shall derive a final answer for tasks faster, possibly with a poor confidence, as the remaining budget does not allow hiring many workers. Figure 2-left shows the evolution of threshold when the ration of solved tasks and the ration of consumed budget evolves. Figure 2-right shows the evolution of threshold when the fraction of budget consumed increased, for several fixed values for the ratio of solved tasks r^q. Each curve in the Figure represents this evolution for a fixed value of r^q. Though function Th^q was chosen arbitrarily, one can notice that its value always lays between 0.5 and 1, decreases with available budget, and increases when the number of remaining tasks diminishes. Observe that when r^q is close to 1, the threshold falls rapidly, as a large number of tasks still has to be evaluated within the remaining budget. On the other hand, when there are less unsolved tasks (e.g. when $r^q = 0.10$), the threshold Th^q decreases slowly.

We can now define a crowdsourcing algorithm (CrowdInc) with a dynamic worker allocation strategy to optimize cost and accuracy. This strategy allocates workers depending on current confidence on final answers, and available resources. CrowdInc is decomposed in two phases, *Estimation* and *Convergence*.

Estimation: As *difficulty* of tasks is not known a priori, the first challenge is to estimate it. To get an initial measure of difficulties, each task needs to be answered by a set of workers. Now, as each worker receives an incentive for a task, this preliminary evaluation has a cost, and finding an optimal number of workers for *difficulty* estimation is a fundamental issue. The initial budget gives some flexibility in the choice of an appropriate number of workers for preliminary evaluation of difficulty. Choosing a random number of workers per task does not seem a wise choice. We choose to devote a fraction of the initial budget to this estimation phase. We devote one third of the total budget ($B_0/3$) to the

---

Algorithm 2: CrowdInc

Data: A set of tasks $T = \{t_1, \ldots, t_n\}$, a budget $= B_0$
Result: Final Answer: $Y = y_1, \ldots, y_n$, Difficulty: d_j, Expertise: α_i, β_i
1 **Initialization :** Set every d_j, α_i, β_i to a random value in $[0, 1]$.
2 $T_{avl} = T$; $q = 0$; $B = B - (B_0/3)$; $B_c = B_0/3$; $r = (B_0/3)/n$
3 //Initial Estimation:
4 Allocate r workers to each task in T_{avl} and get their answers
5 Estimate $d_j^q, \alpha_i^q, \beta_i^q, \hat{c}_j^q, 1 \le j \le n, 1 \le i \le B_0/3$ using EM aggregation
6 Compute the stopping threshold Th^q.
7 **for** $j = 1, \ldots, n$ **do**
8 | **if** $\hat{c}_j^q > Th^q$ **then** $T_{avl} = T \setminus \{j\}$;
9 **end**
10 //Convergence:
11 **while** $(B > 0)$ && $(T_{avl} \ne \emptyset)$ **do**
12 | $q = q + 1$; $l = |T_{avl}|$
13 | Allocate $\mathbf{a}_1^q, \ldots, \mathbf{a}_l^q$ workers to tasks $t_1, \ldots t_l$ based on difficulty.
14 | Get the corresponding answers by all the newly allocated workers.
15 | Estimate $d_j^q, \alpha_i^q, \beta_i^q, \hat{c}_j^q$ using aggregation model.
16 | $B = B - \sum\limits_{i \in 1..|T_{avl}|} \mathbf{a}_i^q$
17 | Compute the stopping threshold Th^q
18 | **for** $j = 1, \ldots, n$ **do**
19 | | **if** $\hat{c}_j^q > Th^q$ **then** $T_{avl} = T_{avl} \setminus \{j\}$;
20 | **end**
21 **end**

---

estimation phase. It leaves a sufficient budget $(2 \cdot B_0/3)$ for the convergence phase. Experiments in the next section show that this seems a sensible choice. After collection of answers for each task, we apply the EM based aggregation technique of Sect. 3 to estimate the *difficulty* of each task as well as the *expertise* of each worker. Considering this as an initial round $q = 0$, we let d_j^0 denote the initially estimated difficulty of each task j, α_i^0, β_i^0 denote the expertise of each worker and y_j^0 denote the aggregated answer for task t_j after the estimation phase. Note that if the difficulty of some tasks is available a priori and is provided by the client, we may skip the estimation step. However, in general clients do not possess such information and this initial step is crucial in estimation of parameters. After this initial estimation, one can already compute Th^0 and decide to stop evaluation of tasks with a sufficient confidence level.

Convergence: The *difficulty* of task d_j^q and the set of remaining tasks T_{avl} are used at each iteration of the convergence phase. Now as the difficulty of each task is estimated, we can use the estimated difficulty d_j^q to allocate the workers dynamically. The number of workers allocated at round $q > 0$ follows a difficulty aware *worker allocation* policy. At each round, we allocate $\mathbf{a}_j^q$ workers to remaining task t_j. This allocation policy guarantees that each remaining task is allocated at least one worker, at most τ workers, and that the more difficult

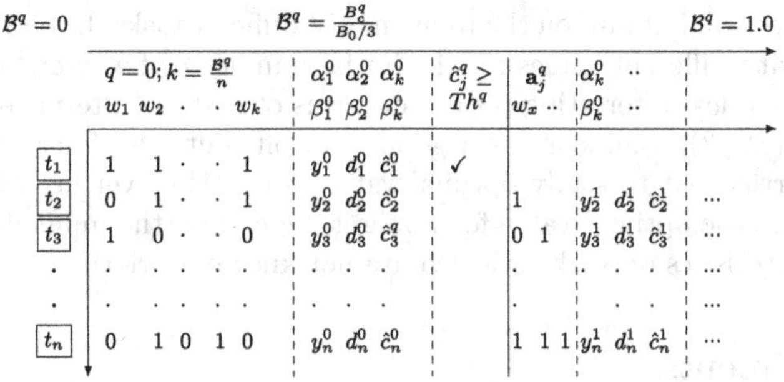

$$B^q = 0 \qquad\qquad B^q = \frac{B^q}{B_0/3} \qquad\qquad B^q = 1.0$$

	$q = 0; k = \frac{B^q}{n}$ $w_1\ w_2\ \cdot\ \cdot\ w_k$	$\alpha_1^0\ \alpha_2^0\ \alpha_k^0$ $\beta_1^0\ \beta_2^0\ \beta_k^0$	$\hat{c}_j^q \geq$ Th^q	a_j^q $w_x\ \cdot\cdot$	$\alpha_k^0\ \cdot\cdot$ $\beta_k^0\ \cdot\cdot$	
t_1	1 1 · · 1	$y_1^0\ d_1^0\ \hat{c}_1^0$	✓			
t_2	0 1 · · 1	$y_2^0\ d_2^0\ \hat{c}_2^0$		1	$y_2^1\ d_2^1\ \hat{c}_2^1$	···
t_3	1 0 · · 0	$y_3^0\ d_3^0\ \hat{c}_3^q$		0 1	$y_3^1\ d_3^1\ \hat{c}_3^1$	···
·						···
·						···
t_n	0 1 0 1 0	$y_n^0\ d_n^0\ \hat{c}_n^0$		1 1 1	$y_n^1\ d_n^1\ \hat{c}_n^1$	···

Fig. 3. A possible state for Algorithm 2

tasks (i.e. tasks that have the more disagreement) are allocated more workers than easier tasks.

Algorithm 2 gives a full description of CrowdInc. We also show the information memorized at each step of the algorithm in Fig. 3. Consider a set of n tasks that have to be annotated with a Boolean tag in $\{0, 1\}$. CrowdInc starts with the *Estimation* phase and allocates k workers for an initial evaluation round ($q = 0$). After collection of answers, and then at each round $q > 0$, we first apply EM based aggregation to estimate the difficulty d_j^q of each of task $t_j \in T_{avl}$, the confidence $\hat{c}_j^q$ in final aggregated answer y_j^q, and the expertise α_i^q, β_i^q of the workers. Then, we use the stopping threshold to decide whether we need more answers for each task. If $\hat{c}_j^q$ is greater than Th^q, the task t_j is removed from T_{avl}. This stopping criterion hence takes a decision based on the confidence in the final answers for a task and on the remaining budget. Consider, in the example of Fig. 3 that the aggregated answer for task t_1 has high confidence, and that $\hat{c}_1^q \geq Th^q$. Then, t_1 does not need further evaluation, and is removed from T_{avl}. Once all tasks solved at round q have been removed, we allocate a_j^q workers to each remaining task t_j in T_{avl} following our difficulty aware policy. Note that, each task gets a different number of workers based on task difficulty. The algorithm stops when either the whole budget B_0 is exhausted or there is no unsolved task left. It then returns the set of all aggregated answers $Y = \{y_j^q \mid 1 \leq j \leq n\}$.

Let us stress an important point of the algorithm. The initial estimation phase (lines 1 to 9) is a standard static allocation, but uses only a limited fraction of the allowed budget. Dynamic allocation depending on confidence in aggregated results only starts from line 10. This initialization phase guarantees that all records are evaluated by at least $r = (B_0/3)/n$ workers, and hence that the algorithm terminates with an answer for each record. Termination of the loop on lines 11 to 21 is guaranteed because the available budget decreases at each round. Consistently, when the whole budget is consumed, the threshold computed at the end of a round is $1/2$. As every aggregated answer achieves a confidence score higher that random guesses, threshold also helps termination. The algorithm is hence guaranteed to terminate in $O((B_0/3)/n + (2.B_0/3))$ rounds. Hence, each record receives between r and $2 \cdot B_0/3 + r$ answers, depending on the difficulty of tagging this record, but also on the frequency of difficult tasks. Experiments were carried out with different values for the initial number r of workers allocated to a task, but gave less interesting results in terms of cost or in terms of accuracy. Setting $r = (B_0/3)/n$ appears as a good tradeoff, but additional experiments should be carried out to study optimal values for r. However, as very often in crowdsourcing, the optimal value for r might depend on the input dataset, and on the characteristics of workers which are not known a priori.

5   Experiments

We evaluate the algorithm on three public available datasets, namely the Product Identification [21], Duck Identification [23] and Sentiment Analysis [15] benchmarks. We briefly detail each dataset and the corresponding tagging tasks. All tags appearing in the benchmarks were collected via Amazon Mechanical Turk. In the **Product Identification** use case, workers were asked to decide whether a *product-name* and a *description* refer to the same product. The answer returned is *True* or *False*. There are 8315 samples and each of them was evaluated by 3 workers. The total number of unique workers is 176 and the total number of answers available is 24945. In the **Duck Identification** use case, workers had to decide if sample images contain a duck. The total number of tasks is 108 and each task was allocated to 39 workers. The total number of unique workers is 39 and the total number of answers is 4212. In the **Sentiment Analysis** use case, workers had to annotate movie reviews as Positive or Negative opinions. The total number of tasks was 500. Each task was given to 20 unique workers and a total number of 143 workers were involved, resulting in a total number of 10000 answers. All these information are synthesized in Table 1.

Table 1. Datasets description.

Dataset	Number of Tasks	Number of tasks with ground truth	Total Number of answers provided by the crowd	Average number of answers for each task	Number of unique crowd workers
Product Identification	8315	8315	24945	3	176
Duck Identification	108	108	4212	39	39
Sentiment Analysis	500	500	10000	20	143

Evaluation of Aggregation: We first compared our aggregation technique to several methods: MV, D&S [3], GLAD [24], PMCRH [12], LFC [17], and Zen-Crowd [4]. We ran the experiment 30 times with different initial values for tasks difficulty and workers expertise. The standard deviation over all the iteration was less than 0.05%. Hence our aggregation is insensitive to initial prior values. We now compare *Recall*, *Specificity* and *Balanced Accuracy* of all methods. The

Table 2. Comparison of EM + aggregation (with Recall, specificity & task difficulty) with MV, D&S, GLAD, PMCRH, LFC, ZenCrowd.

Methods	Recall	Specificity	Balanced Accuracy	Methods	Recall	Specificity	Balanced Accuracy
MV	0.56	0.91	0.73	MV	0.61	0.93	0.77
D&S [3]	0.81	0.93	0.87	D&S [3]	0.65	0.97	0.81
GLAD [24]	0.47	0.98	0.73	GLAD [24]	0.48	0.98	0.73
PMCRH [12]	0.58	0.95	0.76	PMCRH [12]	0.61	0.93	0.77
LFC [17]	0.87	0.91	0.89	LFC [17]	0.64	0.97	0.81
ZenCrowd [4]	0.39	0.98	0.68	ZenCrowd [4]	0.51	0.98	0.75
EM + recall, specificity & difficulty	**0.89**	**0.91**	**0.90**	EM + recall, specificity & difficulty	**0.77**	**0.90**	**0.83**

(a) Duck Identification   (b) Product Identification

Methods	Recall	Specificity	Balanced Accuracy
MV	0.93	0.94	0.4
D&S [3]	0.94	0.94	0.94
GLAD [24]	0.94	0.94	0.94
PMCRH [12]	0.93	0.95	0.94
LFC [17]	0.94	0.94	0.94
ZenCrowd [4]	0.94	0.94	0.94
EM + recall, specificity & difficulty	**0.94**	**0.95**	**0.94**

(c) Sentiment Analysis

results are shown in Table 2. The recall and specificity measures presented in the table characterize the success rate of algorithms on tasks with ground truth 1 and 0 respectively. Balanced Accuracy is the average of recall and specificity (we choose this average to get unbiased estimates on unbalanced dataset). We can observe in Table 2 that our method outperforms other techniques in Duck Identification, Product Identification, and is comparable for Sentiment Analysis.

Evaluation of CrowdInc: The goal of the next experiment was to verify that the cost model proposed in CrowdInc achieves at least the same accuracy but with a smaller budget. We have used Duck identification and Sentiment Analysis for this test. We did not consider the Product Identification benchmark: indeed, as shown in Table 1, the Product Identification associates only 3 answers to each task. This does not allow for a significant experiment with CrowdInc. We compared the performance (cost and accuracy) of CrowdInc to other approaches. The results are given in Fig. 4. Static(MV) denotes the traditional static allocation used in crowdsourcing platforms with majority voting as aggregation technique and Static(EM) denotes a static allocation combined with a more advanced EM based aggregation technique. Both algorithms allocate all the workers (and hence use all their budget) at the beginning of the crowdsourcing process. Considering these two algorithms allows to highlight the impact of EM and of dynamic allocation on cost and accuracy.

The following observation can be made from Fig. 4. First, CrowdInc achieves better accuracy than a static(MV) approach. This is not a real surprise, as MV already showed bad accuracy in Table 2. Then, CrowdInc achieves almost the same accuracy as a Static(EM) based approach in Duck identification, and the same accuracy in Sentiment Analysis. Last, CrowdInc uses a smaller budget than static approaches in all cases.

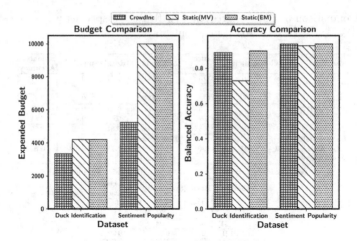

Fig. 4. Comparison of cost vs. Accuracy.

Table 3 shows the time (in seconds) needed by each algorithm to aggregate answers. Static(MV) is the fastest solution: it is not surprising, as the complexity is linear in the number of answers. We recall however that MV has the worst accuracy of all tested aggregation techniques. We have tested aggregation with EM when the number of workers is fixed a priori and is the same for all tasks (Static(EM)). CrowdInc uses EM, but on a dynamic sets of workers and tasks, stopping easiest tasks first. This results in a longer calculus, as EM is used several times on sets of answers of growing sizes. The accuracy of *static(EM)* and CrowdInc are almost the same. Aggregation with CrowdInc takes approximately 11% longer than *static(EM)* but for a smaller budget, as shown in the Fig. 4. To summarize the CrowdInc aggregation needs more time and a smaller budget to aggregate answers with a comparable accuracy. In general, clients using crowd-sourcing services can wait several days to see their task completed. Hence, when time is not a major concern, CrowdInc is hence a sensible solution to reduce the cost of crowdsourcing.

Table 3. Running time (in seconds) of CrowdInc, static MV and Static EM.

Dataset/Methods	CrowdInc	Static(EM)	Static(MV)
Duck Identification	843.26	106.81	0.073
Sentiment Analysis	1323.35	137.79	0.102

6   Spammer Detection

In the preceding sections, we have considered faithful workers, i.e., workers that do their best to return an answer that is, up to their knowledge, the right answer. Some workers may have low competences, but our experimentation showed that despite errors, Crowdink achieves good accuracy. The reason is that workers are usually competent, and that a limited number of errors per question can be compensated by correct answers. Indeed, in a context where workers are faithful, the largest probability for an individual wrong answer is 0.5, as for incompetent workers, answers are almost a random guess. Now, the probability for k wrong answers for a task, and the probability of k consecutive wrong answers by the same worker are very small (0.5^k). Hence, the high probability that individual errors are corrected by other answers allows to achieve good recall and specificity. This setting is completely changed if a worker returns wrong answer with a higher probability, either because he is only interested in incentives, and does not really perform the task he was hired for, but rather returns fast thoughtless answers, or because he is trying to influence the results or accuracy of the crowdsourcing platform. In the rest of this section we consider these two types of spammers, and study the impact of growing proportions of these malevolent workers on the overall accuracy of our algorithm. One can expect crowdsourcing to be robust to a single spammer, but a major danger for a platform is to hire too many spammers. An important parameter to know is hence the maximal percentage of spammers that a platform can accept. A second important parameter is how malevolent workers affect costs of our aggregation algorithm. As shown in Sect. 5, our algorithm allows to save costs when confidence in aggregated answers is sufficient. Now, as malevolence affects answers, it can also reduce confidence in aggregated answers, and subsequently increase the budget spent to reach a consensus. In the rest of this section, we propose a model for several types of spammers, and present the results of experiments showing the maximal percentage of spammers that CrowdInc can accept, and the impact of these spammers on costs.

6.1 Spammers Models

We distinguish several types of spammers, with different motivations and hence different behaviors. For some of them, the objective is to earn fast money by performing a maximal number of tasks within the shortest possible time. For others, the objective is to perturb the system, and reduce its overall efficiency and quality. Last, some spammers want to influence the results returned by the crowdsourcing platform. We distinguish these three types of spammer, and for each type define a particular generating function (i.e., a probability law) for returned answers. Our spammer are represented as follows:

- **Type 1 spammers:** The objective of these spammers is to earn money easily through obfuscated use of crowdsourcing platforms. They do not want to spend time thinking on problems posted on the crowdsourcing platform. They favor easy tasks with a small and finite number of answers and answer as fast as possible to gain the incentives given for task completion. These greedy spammers can be seen as returning a random answer. To fight this type of spam, platforms separate rewards in two parts: the first one for accepting to realize a task, and the second for a correct answer (or at least an answer that conforms with the aggregated result obtained from the set of answers of all workers contributing to the task). Another way to avoid greedy spammers is to select workers only after unpaid qualification tests before allowing them to contribute to paid tasks. Greedy spammers are often reluctant to pass these tests that result in a loss of time, and systematically disqualify them if they answer randomly. The answering profile of a greedy spammer is a profile where the probability to answer x when the ground truth is x is a constant 0.5, regardless of the difficulty of the task. Using the same parameters as for standard workers proposed in Sect. 3, the generative functions for Type 1 spammers are:

$$Pr(l_{ij} = y_j | d_j, \alpha_i, y_j = 1) = 0.5 \text{ and } Pr(l_{ij} = y_j | d_j, \beta_i, y_j = 0) = 0.5 \quad (13)$$

- **Type 2 spammers:** the objective of spammers of this type is to impact efficiency of crowdsourcing platforms. If this type of spammer become majoritary in pool of worker, then the accuracy of the platform can be severely compromised. Though we are not aware of denial of service attacks of this form, assuming existence of this type of spammers and considering various proportions of Type 2 spammers is a way to study the *maximal impact* that spammers can have on a system. The generative functions for Type 2 spammers are:

$$Pr(l_{ij} = 0 | d_j, \alpha_i, y_j = 1) = 1 \text{ and } Pr(l_{ij} = 1 | d_j, \beta_i, y_j = 0) = 1 \quad (14)$$

Note that the probabilities of incorrect answers from Type 2 spammers do not depend on their recall or specificity. We hence use this type of spammer as a worst case measure of spammers impact, as answering incorrectly a question supposes the ability to know the correct answer. In some sense, this is a high (but evil) competence level that should be very rare.
- **Type 3 spammers:** the objective of spammers of this type is to force the results returned by a crowdsourcing platform. In [22], attacks of these spammers are called *sybil attacks*. Regardless of the ground truth, these spammers return the same answer. This type of attack is not a purely theoretical view: It was demonstrated that robots had rigged the results of a famous talent show[2] in 2019. The behavior of a Type 3 spammer is to return systematically the answer he wants to see in the aggregated result. For instance, if worker i is a spammer willing to favor answer 1 to question j, his behavior will be defined by the following generative functions.

$$Pr(l_{ij} = 1 | d_j, \alpha_i, y_j = 1) = 1 \text{ and } Pr(l_{ij} = 1 | d_j, \beta_i, y_j = 0) = 1 \quad (15)$$

Of course, one can write symmetric generative functions when the preferred answer of spammer i is 0. Depending on the chosen answer, a spammer will have a good recall and poor specificity, or the converse. We will call Type 3.1 spammers the malevolent workers that want to force the system to return final answer 0, and Type 3.2 spammers the malevolent workers that want to force the system to return final answer 1.

---

[2] https://en.wikipedia.org/wiki/The_Voice_Kids_(Russian_season_6).

We illustrate the generative function for different types of spammers of Fig. 5. We compare the probability of a correct answer when ground truth is 1 (diagram on the left) for an average user which recall is $\alpha = 0.75$. For a genuine worker of this kind, the probability for a correct answer is represented with a mixed line, and decreases to 0.5 while difficulty increases. On the other hand, the probability of a correct answer for Type 1 spammers is always 0.5. One can see on the figure that the difference between Type 1 spammer and genuine user decreases while difficulty increases. Type 2 spammers (intentional wrong answer, represented by yellow line) and Type 3.1 spammers (constant answer 0 represented by a black dotted line) both have a probability 0 to give the correct answer. The diagram on the right represents similar curves when the ground truth is 0 and the specificity of a genuine user is $\beta = 0.75$.

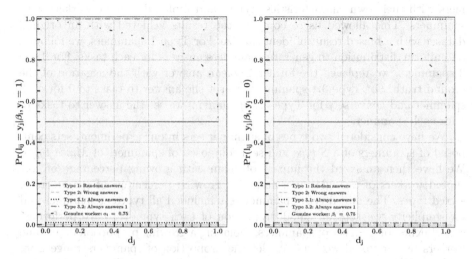

Fig. 5. Generating functions depicting the probability of correct answers for honest workers (with recall $\alpha = 0.75$ and specificity $\beta = 0.75$) and Type 1, Type 2, and Type 3 spammers.

One can notice that the probabilities of correct answers are very different for genuine workers and for spammers. However, detection of a spammer is not as straightforward as Fig. 5 suggests, as ground truth is not known, and correct answers, recalls and specificities are estimated from observed answers.

Though the objective of this section is to study the impact of spammers on efficiency of CrowdInc, one can easily build on the experiments showed later in this section to imagine a simple detection algorithm. Fixing a lower bound $th_R^{l,i}$ and an upper bound $th_R^{u,i}$ for recall (resp. $th_S^{l,i}$ and an upper bound $th_S^{u,i}$ for specificity) for each spammer type i, and claim that a worker w_j is a spammer of type i if $th_R^{l,i} \leq \alpha_j \leq th_R^{u,i}$ and $th_S^{l,i} \leq \beta_j \leq th_S^{u,i}$. Though this algorithm is simplistic, it achieved good detection scores in the experiment showed below.

6.2   Experimentation of CrowdInc with Spammers

The objective of the experiment was to measure the effect of spammers on the performance of our aggregation algorithm, study the impact of spammers on the cost and accuracy and give ways to detect spammers in a pool of workers.

Datasets. We consider the datasets used in Sect. 5, namely *Duck Identification* and *Sentiment Analysis*, and analyze the effect of spammers on CrowdInc's performance. We do not consider the Product Identification dataset as it associates only three unique workers per task. This does not allow conclusive experiments, as replacing a worker by a spammer immediately leads to a situation with 33% of spammers.

The experimentation was organized as follows: we randomly generated spammers with their own characteristics (type), and replaced genuine workers with spammers. This allowed us to compare the results achieved with an original dataset with a biased result of identical size. For Type 1 spammers, we followed an uniform distribution to generate spammers answers for each tasks. For Type 2 spammers, we replaced the former Boolean answer with the negation of the ground truth. For Type 3.1 spammers, we set the answer to tasks to 0 for each spammer and conversely for Type 3.2 spammers, we set the answer to tasks to 1 for each spammer.

We have considered two types of spammer sets in our experiment: sets composed of spammers of a *S type* and sets composed of spammers of *Mixed types*. We have then analyzed the impact of spam with growing percentage of corrupted workers of a single type, and with growing percentage of spammers of mixed types. The mixed type spammer sets included all types of spammer and for simplicity, we kept an equal proportion of each type. We have performed experiments for each set of spammers, replacing a growing proportion of genuine workers by corrupted workers. We let the proportion of spammers range from 10% to 60% to study the effect of spam on the performance of aggregation. Our experiment did not exceed 60% of spammers, because the performance of Crowdinc was already too low with this proportion of spam. Overall, the two datasets and the various composition of genuine workers and spammers sets results in 57 experimentation environments, shown in Table 4. Recall that answers of genuine workers are random values following a probability law, and are sampled according to a profile that depends on workers recall and specificity. This means that the influence of spammers depend on correctness of the answers they returned. We hence ran each experiment 30 times to avoid bias.

6.3   Spammer Detection with Thresholds

One way to detect spammer is to show that they have a poor expertize, than can only be justified by a malevolent behavior. As explained before (see in particular Fig. 5), each spammer type has characteristics that can be observed from the values of recall and specificity. We can hence set thresholds for recall and specificity, and decide by comparing the actual expertize of a worker whether he is a

Table 4. Spam dataset parameters.

Dataset Name	Duck Identification												Sentiment Identification										
Genuine Workers	39												20										
Spammer Type	Individual (Type 1, Type 2, Type 3.1, Type 3.2)						Mixed (Equal number of all type of spammers)						Individual (Type 1, Type 2, Type 3.1, Type 3.2)						Mixed (Equal number of all type of spammers)			
Spam Workers (% compared to genuine workers (approx))	4 (10)	8 (20)	12 (30)	16 (40)	20 (50)	24 (60)	4 (10)	8 (20)	12 (30)	16 (40)	20 (50)	24 (60)	2 (10)	4 (20)	6 (30)	8 (40)	10 (50)	12 (60)	4 (20)	8 (40)	12 (60)		

spammer or not, and even determine the type of spammer that was discovered this way. Now, the difficulty is to set the appropriate values for these thresholds.

We perform a grid search on the values of recall and specificity to find thresholds allowing identification of spammers. We use the Duck identification dataset with 10% of spammer and consider each type of spammer independently. We show the results in Fig. 6. Both recall and specificity range from 0.0 to 1.0. For each plot, the recall value ranges from 0.0 to 1.0 and is represented on the horizontal axis. Likewise, specificity is represented on the y-axis and ranges from 0 to 1. We choose a step size of 0.1 for recall and specificity. Each cell hence represent an interval of values for recall and specificity. The obtained grid is hence a 10×10 grid. Now for each cell, we compute a *detection score*.

Let n_s be the total number of spammers, n_g be the number of genuine workers, n_s^d the number of spammers detected as spammers and n_g^d the number of genuine workers classified as genuine by some spammer detection technique. Then the detection score is

$$\frac{1}{2} \cdot \left(\frac{n_g^d}{n_g} + \frac{n_s^d}{n_s} \right)$$

The maximal detection scores reached for the most accurate thresholds are rather high (above 90%), but do not achieve a 100% correct classification of workers. The graphics of Fig. 6 shows the achieved detection score with a color. For Type 1 spammers, we achieve the best detection score when the recall and specificity values ranges between 0.45 and 0.60. As Type 1 spammers make a random guess to return their answers, their recall and specificity lie between 0.45 and 0.60. This is below the values achieved by the complete pool of genuine honest workers (0.89 and 0.90) in the experiment of Sect. 5. The Type 2 spammer always gives wrong answers. This results in a low value of recall and specificity. We can observe that the detection score to correctly detect Type 2 spammers is high with a threshold for recall and specificity set to 0.2 (or less). The Type 3.1 spammers always return answer 0. In this case, the specificity value is very high, however, the recall value is very low. We can observe that, with a very high specificity threshold > 0.9 and a small recall threshold < 0.2, we get the highest detection score for Type 3.1 spammers. Conversely, the Type 3.2 spammers always answer 1 that leads to very high recall and low specificity. The score to detect Type 3.2 spammers is highest when we have a threshold for recall set to > 0.9 and a threshold for specificity < 0.2.

Overall, the experiments conducted allowed to find appropriate thresholds for detection of all spammers. The optimal synthesized values of thresholds allowing to detect spammers of each category are represented in Table 5.

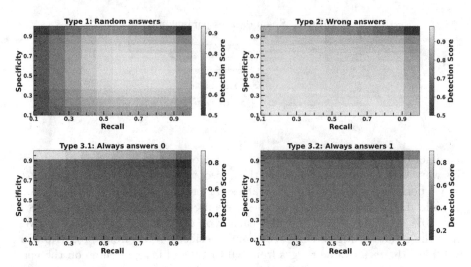

Fig. 6. Threshold search to detect spammers for four spammers type: Type 1, Type 2, Type 3.1 and 3.2.

Table 5. Thresholds to detect spammers of Type 1, Type 2, Type 3.1 and 3.2.

Recall Value Threshold	Specificity Value Threshold	Spammer Type	Description
Low ($0.45 \leq \alpha \leq 0.60$)	Low ($0.45 \leq \beta \leq 0.60$)	Type 1	Random answers
Very low ($\alpha \leq 0.2$)	Very low ($\beta \leq 0.2$)	Type 2	Wrong answers
Very low ($\alpha \leq 0.2$)	High ($0.9 \leq \beta$)	Type 3.1	Always answer 0
High ($0.9 \leq \alpha$)	Very low ($\beta \leq 0.2$)	Type 3.2	Always answers 1

6.4   Effect of Spammers on Accuracy

We now analyze the effect of spammers on accuracy of aggregation. We consider spammer sets composed of spammers of a single type and spammer sets with mixed types. In each experiment, we increase the percentage of spammers from 10% to 60% and use the CrowdInc algorithm proposed in Sect. 4 to aggregate the answers. We do not consider cases with more than 60% of spammers because accuracy is already very low with this percentage of malevolent workers. Let us recall that the achieved recall, specificity and global accuracy achieved by CrowdInc are respectively 0.89, 0.91 and 0.9 for Duck Identification, and 0.94, 0.95 and 0.94 for Sentiment Analysis. We observe the following outcomes.

Unsurprisingly, introducing spammers degrades the overall accuracy of aggregation. This was expected as the spammers, unlike genuine workers whose answer are based on their belief, try to trick the system. Additionally, as the number of spammer increases accuracy of aggregation decreases. This result follows intuition: as more spammers try to trick the system, confidence in aggregated answers decreases. This tendency was visible in all simulation environments. The accuracies, recalls and specificities achieved with 10% spammers are shown in Figs. 7, 8, 9, 10, 11, 12, 13, and 14.

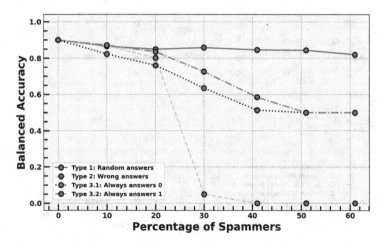

Fig. 7. Effect of individual type spammers: Type 1, Type 2, Type 3.1 and Type 3.2 on balanced accuracy for Duck Identification dataset.

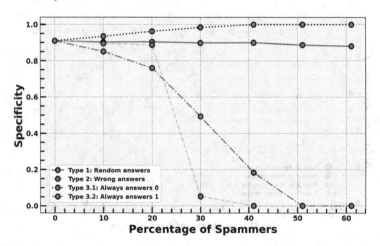

Fig. 8. Effect of individual type spammers: Type 1, Type 2, Type 3.1 and Type 3.2 on specificity for Duck Identification dataset.

Let us discuss more precisely the obtained results for each spammer type. For Type 1 spammers, accuracy falls steadily as shown in Fig. 7 and 10. The Type 1 spammers give random answers, and in this case still have a sufficient probability to return a correct answer. Such a type of spammer affects the overall accuracy of the system very gradually, as their disagreement is easily corrected by genuine workers. All graphics (Figs. 7, 8, 9, 10, 11, 12) show that one can still achieve an acceptable accuracy, recall and specificity with up to 60% of workers returning random answers.

On the other hand, for Type 2 spammers, accuracy decreases very quickly. Observe the results in Fig. 7. With only 20% of Type 2 spammers, accuracy is

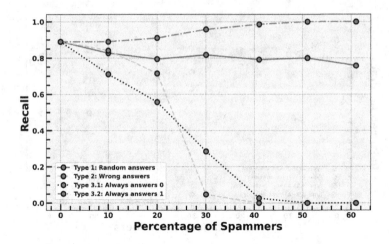

Fig. 9. Effect of individual type spammers: Type 1, Type 2, Type 3.1 and Type 3.2 on recall for Duck Identification dataset.

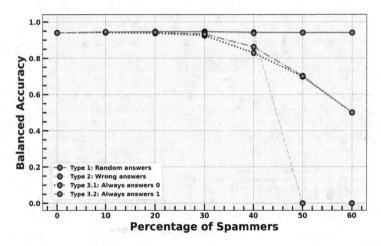

Fig. 10. Effect of individual type spammers: Type 1, Type 2, Type 3.1 and Type 3.2 on balanced accuracy for Sentiment Analysis dataset.

already very low, and with 30% of spammers, the performance of the system is close to 0. The reason is that Type 2 spammers always return a wrong answer, and hence influence the final result. The recall and specificity for Duck Identification Fig. 8 and 9 show the same trend: a proportion of 30% of spammers make the system unusable. For Sentiment Analysis (Figs. 10, 11, 12), the limit lays a little further, allowing up to 40% of corrupted workers.

For Type 3.1 and Type 3.2 accuracy falls gradually as shown in Fig. 7, 10. Note that, such spammers affect negatively the balanced results when most of the tasks have ground truth as 0 and on the contrary affect it positively the ground truth is 1 for a majority of workers. Indeed, specificity of aggregated

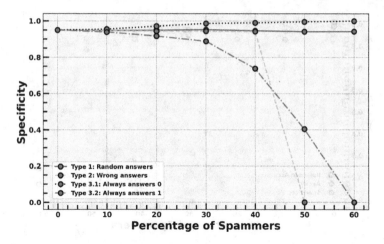

Fig. 11. Effect of individual type spammers: Type 1, Type 2, Type 3.1 and Type 3.2 on specificity for Sentiment Analysis dataset.

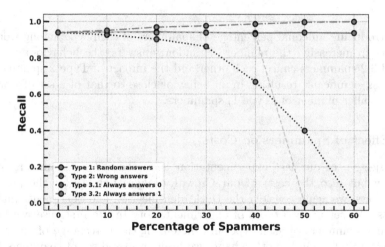

Fig. 12. Effect of individual type spammers: Type 1, Type 2, Type 3.1 and Type 3.2 on recall for Sentiment Analysis dataset.

answers with Type 3.1 spammers approaches 1 (refer Fig. 8, 11) and the recall falls to 0 (refer Fig. 9, 12) when the number of spammers increases. This behavior is expected as Type 3.1 spammers always return answer 1 (and hence achieve 100% correct answers on images with ducks). Symmetric results are obtained with Type 3.2 spammers as depicted in Figs. 8 and 9.

Let us now consider mixed set of spammers. We introduced an equal share of spammers of each type and incrementally increased the percentage of spammers among workers. We find that in this case, recall, specificity and the balanced accuracy falls gradually as shown in Figs. 13 and 14. An intuitive explanation is

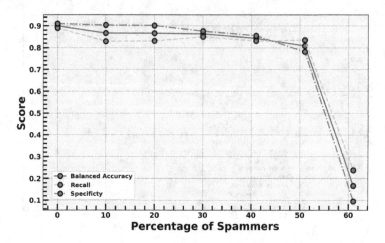

Fig. 13. Effect of Mixed spammers: equally distributed Type 1, Type 2, Type 3.1 and Type 3.2 for Duck Identification dataset.

that introducing an equal percentage of spammers of each type among workers amounts to increasing the number of random answers: the behaviors of Type 3.1 and 3.2 spammers cancel each other and the impact of Type 2 spammers is hence less significant, resulting in an behavior close to that of a set of workers with a smaller number of (Type 1) spammers.

6.5   Effect of Spammers on Costs

The objective of our last experimentation is to study how spammers affect accuracy but also the costs of our CrowdInc algorithm. As for the previous experiments, we again consider the Duck Identification and Sentiment Analysis datasets. We set up two types of experimentation. In the first case, we insert individual spammers of each type and increment the percentage of spammers from 10% to 60%. On the other hand, we insert a mixed set of spammers with an equal proportion of spammers of all type. Here, we also insert spammers incrementally from 10% to 60%. We compare the performance of CrowdInc to varying degree of spammers in both cases.

We first show compared costs and accuracies for sets of spammers of a single type, for growing ratios of malevolent workers. We show the achieved results for Duck Identification in Fig. 15 and Sentiment Analysis in Fig. 16. In each Figure, the top left bar plot represents the cost, the top right bar plot represents the accuracy, the bottom left bar plot represents the specificity and the bottom right bar plot represents the recall, for each spammer type and for varying percentages of spammers. Let us first consider Duck Identification (Fig. 15). For Type 1 spammers, the cost of aggregation increases with the percentage of spammers, while accuracy, specificity and recall remain quite stable. The explanation is that, when spammers give random answers they may be correct or wrong. Such

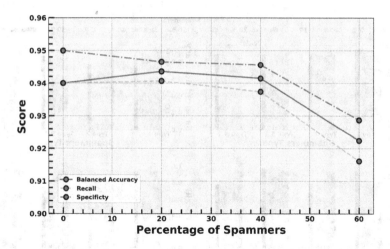

Fig. 14. Effect of Mixed spammers: equally distributed Type 1, Type 2, Type 3.1 and Type 3.2 for Sentiment Analysis dataset.

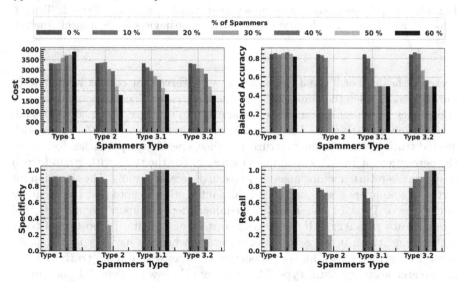

Fig. 15. Comparison of cost vs. accuracy (Individual Spammers): Type 1, Type 2, Type 3.1 and Type 3.2 with varying percentage of spammers for Duck Identification dataset.

random answering by workers increases the number of steps needed to converge to a final consensual answer, but one error compensates the other, and the final results are not affected. The Type 2 spammers provide always incorrect answers. We observe that in Duck Identification, the cost decreases as well as accuracy, recall and specificity (which are almost 0 and not visible on plots for a percentage of spammer $\geq 40\%$). Note that compared to Type 1 spammer, performance

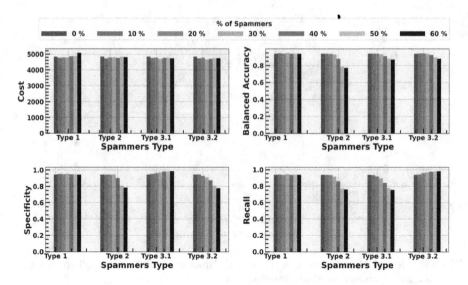

Fig. 16. Comparison of cost vs. accuracy (Individual Spammers): Type 1, Type 2, Type 3.1 and Type 3.2 with varying percentage of spammers for Sentiment Analysis dataset.

decreases faster. For Type 3.1 spammers, we observe that cost as well as accuracy decreases when the number of spammers increases. Specificity increases and approaches 1 with a high number of spammers. In contrast, the recall values fall very sharply and reach 0. The intuitive reason is the following: for tasks with ground truth is, the spammers return 1. Hence, specificity approaches to 1 when the percentage of Type 3.1 spammers increases. For the tasks with ground truth 0, spammers return a wrong answer, so recall decreases rapidly. The situation for Type 3.2 spammers is symmetric. It is also interesting to note that the accuracy in the case of Type 3.1 and Type 3.2 spammers depends upon the proportion of ground truth with 0 or 1. If the dataset consists of a greater proportion of tasks with ground truth 0, we get greater accuracy when we have Type 3.1 spammers. In contrast with a higher proportion of tasks with ground truth as 1, we get greater accuracy with Type 3.2 spammers than with Type 3.1 spammers. Though it might be intriguing that cost decreases with Type 2, Type 3.1 and Type 3.2 spammers, there is an intuitive explanation: as spammers all provide the same biased answer, they allow to reach a (possibly wrong) consensus within a smaller number of rounds. For Sentiment Analysis, the costs remain almost stable, while accuracy decreases. In fact, even when the number of spammers increases, the impact on cost and accuracy also depends upon how the genuine workers are answering. If there is a lot of agreement among the answers provided by the genuine workers, the impact of spammers on cost and accuracy is limited. In the case of Sentiment Analysis, there is a lot of agreement among workers answers. As a result, the effect of spammers answers is lighter than for the Duck Identification dataset.

Let us now analyze results for a mixed set of spammers with an equal proportion of each spammer type. We find that when the percentage of spammers increases, the cost of CrowdInc increases and the performance metrics (accuracy, specificity and recall) decrease. The results are shown in Fig. 17 and 18. As explained earlier, mixed composition of spammer sets shows identical performance as spammers sets with only Type 1 spammers. Here also, changes in cost and accuracy depend on answers of genuine workers. As a result, we can observe that the effect of spammers is less important on the Sentiment Analysis dataset than on the Duck Identification dataset. This observation extends to costs.

Overall, the experimentation showed a very marginal increase is the cost of CrowdInc (and hence also on the number of rounds) for a percentage of spammers below 20%. Accuracy of answers is still good with 20% of spammers of all types. This means that Crowding stops with a confidence in forged data that is still high. Accuracy starts to fall dramatically (and costs starts to increase) for Duck Identification with 30% of spammers, while results are still acceptable with 40% of spammers with Sentiment Analysis. This shows that spammer impact, just like performance of aggregation mechanisms, is data-dependent. Though it is difficult to find general rules explaining this difference, one can notice that the number of answers in Sentiment Analysis is larger. An hypothesis is that it makes this dataset more robust to changes introduced by malevolent workers. Following the remarks in [26], who concluded that there is not aggregation technique that can be considered as the ultimate one, we believe that spammer sensitivity is a parameter that may vary with size and difficulty of data. This is not only a characteristics of data, but also of workers culture and beliefs: [23] showed

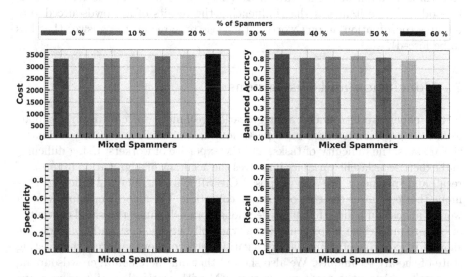

Fig. 17. Comparison of cost vs. accuracy (Mixed Spammers): equally distributed Type 1, Type 2, Type 3.1 and Type 3.2 with varying percentage of spammers for Duck Identification dataset.

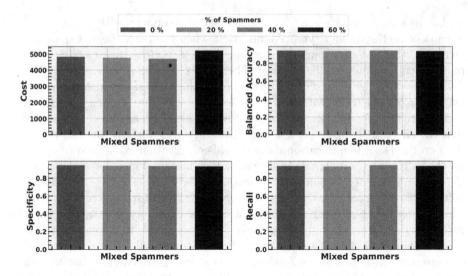

Fig. 18. Comparison of cost vs. accuracy (Mixed Spammers): equally distributed Type 1, Type 2, Type 3.1 and Type 3.2 with varying percentage of spammers for Sentiment Analysis dataset.

on the Duck Identification dataset that workers had difficulties to differentiate ducks and grebes, due to a cultural habit associating ducks with a short neck. Yet, a general tendency showed by our experiment is that Type 1 spammers (returning random answers) have little effect on accuracy of the results. This is good news, as it means that influencing the results of a crowdsourced vote requires coordination among workers (at least to agree on the answer that has to be forced).

7   Conclusion and Discussions

In this paper, we introduced an aggregation technique for crowdsourcing platforms. Aggregation is based on expectation maximization and jointly estimates the answers, the difficulty of tasks, and the expertise of workers. Using difficulty and expertise as latent variables improves the accuracy of aggregation in terms of recall and specificity. We also proposed CrowdInc an incremental labeling technique that optimizes the cost of answers collection. The algorithm implements a worker allocation policy that takes decisions from a dynamic threshold computed at each round, which helps achieving a trade off between cost and accuracy. We showed in experiments that our aggregation technique outperforms the existing state-of-the-art techniques. We also showed that our incremental crowdsourcing approach achieves the same accuracy as EM with static allocation of workers, better accuracy than majority voting, and in both cases at lower costs.

In a second part of the paper, we have studied the impact of malevolent workers on performance of CrowdInc. In the considered cases, our algorithm can accept 10 to 20% of spammers without affecting too much its accuracy and cost. As answering profiles of spammers are rather different from standard behaviors, one can rely on recall and specificity estimation to detect spammers when the percentage of corrupted workers is not too high.

The ideas proposed in this paper can lead to several improvements that will be considered in future work. In the paper, we addressed binary tasks for simplicity, but the approach can be easily extended to tasks with a finite number m of answers. For each worker i, and for a given difficulty, one can specify the joint probability of ground truth $y_j = v$ and of an answer $L_{ij} = v' \in \{1, \ldots, m\}$ for $v, v' \in \{1, \ldots, m\}$. The role of the EM algorithm remains to estimate the ground truth and parameters such as task difficulty and workers expertise. The difficulty of each task t_j remains a parameter d_j. Expertise is the ability to classify a task as m when its ground truth is m. An EM algorithm just has to consider probabilities of the form $Pr(L_{ij} = v' | y_j = v, \alpha_i, \beta_i, d_j)$ to derive hidden parameters and final labels for each task. Another easy improvement is to consider incentives that depend on workers accuracy. This can be done with a slight adaptation of costs in the CrowdInc algorithm. Another possible improvement is to try to hire experts when the synthesized difficulty of a task is high, to avoid hiring numerous workers or increase the number of rounds.

Last, we think that the complexity of CrowdInc can be improved. The complexity of each E-step of the aggregation is linear in the number of answers. The M-step maximizes the log likelihood with an iterative process (truncated Newton algorithm). However, the E and M steps have to be repeated many times. The cost of this iteration is visible in Table 3, where one clearly see the difference of running time between a linear approach such as Majority Voting (third column), a single round of EM (second column), and CrowdInc. Using CrowdInc to reduce costs results in an increased duration to compute final answers. Indeed, the calculus performed at round i to compute hidden variables for a task t is lost at step $i + 1$ if t is not stopped. An interesting idea is to consider how a part of computations can be reused from a round to the next one to speed up convergence. However, building an incremental version of EM is far from being trivial. Indeed, EM converges towards optima, that can sometimes be local. It is known that the choice of initial values for hidden parameters need not influence the final result. One can, for instance, reuse the recall and specificity computed for workers in a round, and expect this quality to remains stable in subsequent rounds, and hence speed up convergence of EM. However, this particular initialization of round does guarantee improvement of CrowdInc in all cases, and experimental validation is needed to show that, on the average, remembering parameters speeds up convergence.

Acknowledgements. We would like to thank anonymous reviewers for their careful reading and for useful comments on a preliminary version of this work.

References

1. Dai, P., Lin, C.H., Weld, D.S.: POMDP-based control of workflows for crowdsourcing. Artif. Intell. **202**, 52–85 (2013)
2. Daniel, F., Kucherbaev, P., Cappiello, C., Benatallah, B., Allahbakhsh, M.: Quality control in crowdsourcing: a survey of quality attributes, assessment techniques, and assurance actions. ACM Comput. Surv. **51**(1), 7 (2018)
3. Dawid, A.Ph., Skene, A.M.: Maximum likelihood estimation of observer error-rates using the EM algorithm. J. R. Stat. Soc. Ser. C (Appl. Stat.) **28**(1), 20–28 (1979)
4. Demartini, G., Difallah, D.E., Cudré-Mauroux, Ph.: Zencrowd: leveraging probabilistic reasoning and crowdsourcing techniques for large-scale entity linking. In: Proceedings of the 21st World Wide Web Conference (WWW 2012), pp. 469–478. ACM (2012)
5. Dempster, A.P., Laird, N.M., Rubin, D.B.: Maximum likelihood from incomplete data via the EM algorithm. J. Roy. Stat. Soc.: Ser. B (Methodol.) **39**(1), 1–22 (1977)
6. Flach, P.A.: Machine Learning - The Art and Science of Algorithms that Make Sense of Data. Cambridge University Press (2012)
7. Garcia-Molina, H., Joglekar, M., Marcus, A., Parameswaran, A., Verroios, V.: Challenges in data crowdsourcing. Trans. Knowl. Data Eng. **28**(4), 901–911 (2016)
8. Geng, B., Li, Q., Varshney, P.K.: Prospect theory based crowdsourcing for classification in the presence of spammers. IEEE Trans. Signal Process. **68**, 4083–4093 (2020)
9. Halpin, H., Blanco, R.: Machine-learning for spammer detection in crowd-sourcing. In: Proceedings of the 4th Human Computation Workshop, HCOMP@AAAI 2012. AAAI Workshops, vol. WS-12-08. AAAI Press (2012)
10. Karger, D.R., Oh, S., Shah, D.: Iterative learning for reliable crowdsourcing systems. In: Advances in Neural Information Processing Systems 24: 25th Annual Conference on Neural Information Processing Systems (NIPS 2011), pp. 1953–1961 (2011)
11. Le, J., Edmonds, A., Hester, V., Biewald, L.: Ensuring quality in crowdsourced search relevance evaluation: the effects of training question distribution. In: SIGIR 2010 Workshop on Crowdsourcing for Search Evaluation, vol. 2126, pp. 22–32 (2010)
12. Li, Q., Li, Y., Gao, J., Zhao, B., Fan, W., Han, J.: Resolving conflicts in heterogeneous data by truth discovery and source reliability estimation. In: Proceedings of the 2014 ACM SIGMOD International Conference on Management of Data, pp. 1187–1198. ACM (2014)
13. Miao, C., Li, Q., Su, L., Huai, M., Jiang, W., Gao, J.: Attack under disguise: an intelligent data poisoning attack mechanism in crowdsourcing. In: Proceedings of the 2018 World Wide Web Conference on World Wide Web, WWW 2018, pp. 13–22. ACM (2018)
14. Nash, S.G.: Newton-type minimization via the Lanczos method. SIAM J. Numer. Anal. **21**(4), 770–788 (1984)
15. B. Pang and L. Lee. A sentimental education: Sentiment analysis using subjectivity summarization based on minimum cuts. In Proceedings of ACL'04, the 42nd annual meeting on Association for Computational Linguistics, pages 271–278. Association for Computational Linguistics, 2004

16. Raykar, V., Agrawal, P.: Sequential crowdsourced labeling as an epsilon-greedy exploration in a Markov decision process. In: Proceedings of the Seventeenth International Conference on Artificial Intelligence and Statistics. Proceedings of Machine Learning Research, vol. 33, pp. 832–840. PMLR (2014)

17. Raykar, V.C., et al.: Learning from crowds. J. Mach. Learn. Res. **11**(Apr), 1297–1322 (2010)

18. Raykar, V.C., Shipeng, Yu.: Eliminating spammers and ranking annotators for crowdsourced labeling tasks. J. Mach. Learn. Res. **13**(1), 491–518 (2012)

19. Tran-Thanh, L., Venanzi, M., Rogers, A., Jennings, N.R.: Efficient budget allocation with accuracy guarantees for crowdsourcing classification tasks. In: Proceedings of the 12th International conference on Autonomous Agents and Multi-Agent Systems, AAMAS 2013, pp. 901–908. International Foundation for Autonomous Agents and Multiagent Systems (2013)

20. Venanzi, M., Guiver, J., Kazai, G., Kohli, P., Shokouhi, M.: Community-based bayesian aggregation models for crowdsourcing. In: 23rd International World Wide Web Conference, WWW 2014, pp. 155–164. ACM (2014)

21. Wang, J., Kraska, T., Franklin, M.J., Feng, J.: Crowder: crowdsourcing entity resolution. Proc. VLDB Endow. **5**(11), 1483–1494 (2012)

22. Wang, Y., Wang, K., Miao, C.: Truth discovery against strategic sybil attack in crowdsourcing. In: KDD 2020: The 26th ACM SIGKDD Conference on Knowledge Discovery and Data Mining, pp. 95–104. ACM (2020)

23. Welinder, P., Branson, S., Perona, P., Belongie, S.J.: The multidimensional wisdom of crowds. In: Proceedings of NIPS 2010, Advances in Neural Information Processing Systems 23: 24th Annual Conference on Neural Information Processing Systems 2010, pp. 2424–2432. Curran Associates Inc. (2010)

24. Whitehill, J., Wu, T., Bergsma, J., Movellan, J.R., Ruvolo, P.L.: Whose vote should count more: Optimal integration of labels from labelers of unknown expertise. In: Proceedings of NIPS'09, Advances in Neural Information Processing Systems 22: 23rd Annual Conference on Neural Information Processing Systems, pp. 2035–2043. Curran Associates Inc. (2009)

25. Xu, A., Feng, X., Tian, Y.: Revealing, characterizing, and detecting crowdsourcing spammers: a case study in community Q&A. In: Proceedings of INFOCOM 2015, Conference on Computer Communications, pp. 2533–2541. IEEE (2015)

26. Zheng, Y., Li, G., Li, Y., Shan, C., Cheng, R.: Truth inference in crowdsourcing: is the problem solved? Proc. VLDB Endow. **10**(5), 541–552 (2017)

A Partitioning Approach for Skyline Queries in Presence of Partial and Dynamic Orders

Karim Alami$^{(\boxtimes)}$ and Sofian Maabout

Univ. Bordeaux, CNRS, LaBRI, UMR 5800, Talence, France
{karim.alami,maabout}@u-bordeaux.fr

Abstract. Consider the case of tourists looking for flight tickets. While one may assume that every tourist does prefer lower price, the preference among the airline companies is on the one hand *partial*, i.e., some companies may be incomparable, and on the other hand, it is *dynamic* in the sense that users have different preferences among the companies. In this paper, we address the problem of answering skyline queries in the presence of such partially and dynamically ordered attributes. The main idea of our solution consists in decomposing each query into a set of independent sub-queries with respect to the user's preference. Our contribution is twofold: (i) we propose an algorithm exploiting the above property to evaluate skyline queries on the fly and (ii) a pre-materialization of some sub-queries in order to optimize a query workload. We demonstrate empirically the efficiency of our proposals regarding its direct competitors.

Keywords: Skyline queries · Partial and dynamic order · Data partitioning · Materialization

1 Introduction

The skyline operator introduced by [5] is relevant for retrieving the best elements wrt the user preferences. The skyline set with regard to a dataset T represents the set of not *dominated* tuples, i.e., a tuple t belongs to the skyline set if there does not exist any tuple t' which is *better* than or equal (equivalent) to t on all attributes and strictly better on at least one attribute.

Consider Table 1 where information about movies proposed by a *media-services provider* is registered. Movies are described by their *Genre* and critic scores. Metacritic and Rotten Tomatoes are online platforms specialized in rating movies. Audience represents the score given by subscribers. A movie is in the skyline of Table 1 iff there does not exists any other movie better or equal to it wrt all four attributes, and at least strictly better on one attribute. While comparing movies regarding their respective ratings is natural, considering their genre is not immediate. In fact, the order relationship among the values of each attribute's domain is expressed by a set of orders (preference) $\mathcal{R}$.

© Springer-Verlag GmbH Germany, part of Springer Nature 2021
A. Hameurlain et al. (Eds.): TLDKS XLIX, LNCS 12920, pp. 70–96, 2021.
https://doi.org/10.1007/978-3-662-64148-4_3

Two aspects of $\mathcal{R}$ are relevant to skyline queries:

- $\mathcal{R}$ is either total or partial. $\mathcal{R}$ is total when every two values are ordered. Per contra, $\mathcal{R}$ is partial when there exists at least two values which are not comparable. To illustrate, consider Table 1. Metacritic, Tomato and Audience attributes have their respective domain in $\mathbb{N}$. Since larger ratings are preferred, the preference on each of these three attributes is the relation > on $\mathbb{N}$ which is total. By contrast, for Genre attribute, its domain values have not to be totally ordered. E.g., one may prefer comedy over thriller but has no preference between comedy and sci-fi. These two last values are incomparable regarding the user's preference.
- $\mathcal{R}$ can be either static or dynamic. Again, consider Table 1. The orders on Metacritic, Tomato and Audience respective domains are unique and set a priori. While for Genre, the order depends on users preferences. More precisely, during their quest of the *best* movies, users are asked to express their own preference on Genre's domain in terms of an order relation.

Table 1. Movie rating

	Metacritic	Tomato	Audience	Genre
t_1	56	65	85	$c : comedy$
t_2	63	70	75	$s : sci - fi$
t_3	89	80	90	$h : horror$
t_4	70	72	88	$h : horror$
t_5	63	70	50	$r : romance$
t_6	45	42	80	$a : action$
t_7	52	69	75	$t : thriller$
t_8	64	74	52	$c : comedy$
t_9	73	80	90	$s : sci - fi$
t_{10}	81	71	84	$a : acion$

Example 1. Consider Table 1. While the preference on Metacritic, Tomato and Audience attributes is: the higher the score the better the movie. For Genre, there is no a priori preference over the attribute's domain. Users are asked to describe their preferences through a set of value to value comparability. One user preference could be $\mathcal{R} = \{(h, c), (s, t)\}$ which expresses that *horror* is preferred to *comedy*, and *sci-fi* is preferred to *thriller*. This preference makes comparable the movies having *comedy* or *horror* genre, i.e., $\{t_1, t_3, t_4, t_8\}$. Likewise, t_2, t_7, t_9 are comparable because of *sci-fi* and *thriller* genres. The skyline set over the movie dataset by considering the user preference $\mathcal{R}$ expressed above is composed of $\{t_3, t_5, t_9, t_{10}\}$. The remaining tuples are dominated. For example,

- t_1 is not in the skyline because it is dominated by t_3 which has better scores and better genre (*horror* is preferred over *comedy*).
- t_6 is not in the skyline because t_{10} has better scores and both have the same genre *action*. Observe that this genre is not mentioned in $\mathcal{R}$ making t_6 comparable to only those tuples sharing the same genre.

The skyline set changes dramatically with the user preference. Consider $\mathcal{R}' = \{(r,h), (s,h), (c,h), (a,h), (t,h)\}$, i.e. every genre is better than horror. The skyline set is then $\{t_1, t_2, t_3, t_5, t_6, t_7, t_8, t_9, t_{10}\}$. Observe that t_3 belongs to the skyline set despite being a horror movie. This is because t_3 has the higher ratings in the dataset.

Another situation where partial orders should be used is when the user's preference is expressed in terms of a combination of dimensions. The following example illustrates this case.

Example 2. Consider again Table 1 and suppose that in addition, there is a Country dimension. Then users may want to express their preference not just in terms of Genre but in combination with the country. For example, one may prefer Korean romance over British romance and British comedies over Korean comedies. The user preference is then $\mathcal{R} = \{((K,r), (B,r)), ((B,c)(K,c))\}$. In this case, the two dimensions Genre and Country can be seen as a single dimension on which users can define a preference.

Previous work which investigated skyline computation with partially ordered attributes either proposed on the fly algorithms, i.e., computing the query from scratch, or proposed materialization techniques, i.e., precomputing some indexing structures. One of the techniques proposed so far to implement on the fly algorithms is: given a dataset with partially ordered attribute B, transform B into a set of totally ordered virtual attributes $\phi(B)$ and then run state of the art skyline algorithm on the transformed dataset [20]. Finding the minimal number of totally ordered dimensions needed to express a partial order is known to be NP-Hard. So in practice, heuristics are used. Note that skyline computation cost increases wrt the data dimensionality. Regarding materialization techniques, [19] proposed to compute and store the skylines wrt *every* total order over the attribute B. Then answer a query q which considers a preference $\mathcal{R}$ through the stored skylines. Because of the exponential number of the total orders, this solution is practical only for very small domains. Further details about related work and its limitations are provided in Sect. 5.

In this paper we exhibit a couple of properties letting the decomposition of every skyline query q, using a preference $\mathcal{R}$, into a set Q of *independent* sub-queries. The result of q is obtained by just combining the results of the sub-queries $q' \in Q$. Because these queries are independent from each others, they can be executed in parallel. On another side, if all or some of these sub-queries are materialized, the computation time can be optimized.

More specifically, the main contributions of the present work are:

- A novel approach to compute skyline queries with partially and dynamically ordered attributes.

- A materialization technique to optimize our algorithm.
- A workload driven selection of sub-queries to materialize.
- We provide our software[1] to the scientific community.

Paper Organization. The next section presents the main definitions used throughout the paper. Then we present our approach, first, in case of datasets with only one partially ordered attribute. Afterwards, we generalize to the case of multiple attributes. In Sect. 4, we address the sub-queries materialization. Finally, we discuss state of the art and we empirically evaluate our proposals wrt direct competitors.

2 Preliminaries

In this section, we define the main concepts we use throughout the paper which are (i) order, (ii) preference, (iii) dominance, and (iv) skyline query. The context of the problem we study is as follows: we have a set of dimensions (attributes) $\mathcal{D}$ composed of both totally and statically ordered dimensions $\mathcal{A} = \{A_1, \ldots, A_s\}$, and partially and dynamically ordered dimensions $\mathcal{B} = \{B_1, \ldots, B_l\}$. A dataset T over the set of dimensions $\mathcal{D}$. Users are interested in the skyline set of T by considering their preferences over $\{A_1, \ldots, A_s, B_1, \ldots, B_l\}$ domains.

We first define the *order* relation which expresses the user preference between **two values**.

Definition 1. *(Order) Let $D \in \mathcal{D}$, $dom(D)$ denotes its domain, and $d_i, d_j \in dom(D)$. $o = (d_i, d_j)$ is an order which expresses that d_i is preferred over d_j. We use as well the notation $d_i \prec_D d_j$[2].*

Definition 2. *(Preference) Let $D \in \mathcal{D}$. A preference $\mathcal{R}$ over D is a set of orders over $dom(D)$. $\mathcal{R}$ respects the following properties:*

- *transitivity: $(d_i, d_j) \in \mathcal{R}$ and $(d_j, d_k) \in \mathcal{R}$ then $(d_i, d_k) \in \mathcal{R}$.*
- *asymmetry: $(d_i, d_j) \in \mathcal{R}$ then $(d_j, d_i) \notin \mathcal{R}$*

Observe that a preference over an attribute is nothing but a classical partial order relation defined on its domain.

Remark 1. Recall that $\mathcal{D} = \mathcal{A} \cup \mathcal{B}$. Every $A_i \in \mathcal{A}$ is totally and statically ordered. For example, the preference over Tomatoes attribute in Table 1 is the relation $>$ over $\mathbb{N}$. So from now on, we consider only preferences defined on those attributes admitting dynamic partial orders over their respective domains, i.e., $B_i \in \mathcal{B}$.

Example 3. Consider the movie rating in Table 1. A user preference over the attribute **Genre** can be expressed by $\mathcal{R} = \{(c,s),(s,h),(c,h),$ $(c,r),(r,h),(h,t),(s,t),(r,t),(t,a),(s,a),(r,a),(h,a)\}$. Obviously, this preference can be represented by the DAG in Fig. 1.

---

[1] https://github.com/DynamicPartialSky/dySky.
[2] We use the term *order* for ordering just a single pair of values.

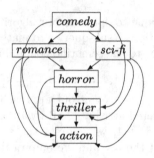

Fig. 1. DAG representation of $\mathcal{R}$

Definition 3 (Dominance). *Let T be a table over $\mathcal{D} = \{A_1, \ldots, A_s, B_1, \ldots, B_l\}$ and let $\mathcal{R} = \{R_1, \ldots, R_l\}$ be a preference over the attributes $B_1, \ldots, B_l$. Let t, t' be two tuples, then t dominates t' iff $t[D] \preceq_D t'[D] \ \forall D \in \mathcal{D}$ and $\exists D \in \mathcal{D}$ such that $t[D] \prec_D t'[D]$. We denote the dominance relation by $t \sqsubset_\mathcal{D} t'$.*

Given a skyline query q, $q.\mathcal{R}$ denotes its related preference $\mathcal{R}$.

Definition 4 (Skyline query). *Given $\mathcal{D}$, T, and a query q. The skyline set $Sky_{q.\mathcal{R}}(T, \mathcal{D}) = \{t \in T \mid \nexists t' \in T \ s.t. \ t' \sqsubset_\mathcal{D} t\}$ is the set of not dominated tuples. We denote also the skyline set by $Sky_{q.\mathcal{R}}(T)$ or simply $Sky_{q.\mathcal{R}}$ when T and/or $\mathcal{D}$ are clear from the context.*

So far, we defined the main concepts in our work. Table 2 summarizes the notations used throughout the paper.

Table 2. Notations

Notation	Definition
$A_1, \ldots, A_s$	Totally ordered attributes
$B_1, \ldots, B_l$	Partially ordered attributes
$\mathcal{D}$	Set of all attributes
T	Dataset over $\mathcal{D}$
m	Size of $dom(B_i) \forall B_i \in \mathcal{B}$
n	Size of T
$\mathcal{R} = \{R_1, \ldots, R_l\}$	Preference over $B_1, \ldots, B_l$
o	An order
q	A skyline query
$q.\mathcal{R}$	Preference of the query q
$Sky_{q.R}(T, D)$	Skyline set wrt q
Q	A workload

In the next section we present the properties of skyline queries that we exploit to devise our solutions.

3   dySky Algorithm

The objective of our work is to efficiently answer skyline queries q wrt user preference $q.\mathcal{R}$ over a dataset T. For the ease of the presentation, first, we consider datasets with only one dynamic dimension.

Our approach is based on the following property: a tuple which does not belong to the skyline set wrt a preference composed of some order in $q.\mathcal{R}$, does not belong to the skyline set wrt $q.\mathcal{R}$. More precisely,

Theorem 1. *Given* $\mathcal{D} = \{A_1, \ldots, A_s, B\}$, *a dataset* T, *and a query* q. *Let* $t \in T$, *then* $t \notin Sky_{q.\mathcal{R}}$ *iff* $\exists o \in q.\mathcal{R}$ *s.t.* $t \notin Sky_{\{o\}}$.

Proof. (i) $t \notin Sky_{q.\mathcal{R}} \Rightarrow \exists o \in q.\mathcal{R}$ s.t. $t \notin Sky_{\{o\}}$: let $t \notin Sky_{q.\mathcal{R}}$ then there exists a tuple t' dominating t such that either (i) $t'[B] = t[B]$ and $t' \prec_A t$ or (ii) $t'[B] \prec_B [B]$ and $t' \preceq_A t$. In the first case t' dominates t whatever the preference $q.\mathcal{R}$ hence $t \notin Sky_{\{o\}} \forall o \in q.\mathcal{R}$. For the second case, $t \notin Sky_{\{(t'[B],t[B])\}}$.

(ii) $\exists o \in q.\mathcal{R}$ s.t. $t \notin Sky_{\{o\}} \Rightarrow t \notin Sky_{q.\mathcal{R}}$: $t \notin Sky_{\{o\}}$ means there exists a tuple t' such that $t' \sqsubset_\mathcal{D} t$. Whatever the remaining orders in $q.\mathcal{R}$, $t' \sqsubset_\mathcal{D} t$.

The above theorem states that a tuple t does not belong to the skyline wrt to a given preference $q.\mathcal{R}$ if and only if t does not belong to the skyline wrt a *singleton* preference composed of some order in $q.\mathcal{R}$.

We introduce here the notation of **complementary** skyline or shortly c-skyline. Given a query q, its c-skyline is $NSky_{q.\mathcal{R}}$, the set of dominated tuples wrt $q.\mathcal{R}$.

To summarize, by computing those tuples not belonging to the skyline wrt every preference composed of some order in $q.\mathcal{R}$, i.e., $NSky_{\{o\}} \forall o \in q.\mathcal{R}$, we deduce $NSky_{q.\mathcal{R}}$ as stipulated in the following corollary.

Corollary 1. *Given a query* q.

$$NSky_{q.\mathcal{R}} = \bigcup_{\forall o \in q.\mathcal{R}} NSky_{\{o\}}$$

Proof. From Theorem 1. Let $t \in T$.

$t \in NSky_{q.\mathcal{R}} \Leftrightarrow t \in NSky_{\{o_1\}} \vee \cdots \vee t \in NSky_{\{o_n\}}$ s.t. $o_1, \ldots, o_n \in q.\mathcal{R}$ then $t \in \bigcup_{\forall o \in q.\mathcal{R}} NSky_{\{o\}}$

Example 4. Consider the movie dataset in Table 1. Given a query q with $q.\mathcal{R} = \{(c,s), (s,h), (c,r), (c,h)\}$ then $NSky_{q.\mathcal{R}} = NSky_{\{(c,s)\}} \cup NSky_{\{(s,h)\}} \cup NSky_{\{(c,r)\}} \cup NSky_{\{(c,h)\}} = \{t_2, t_5\}$.

The skyline is then $T \setminus \{t_2, t_5\} = \{t_1, t_3, t_4, t_6, t_7, t_8, t_9, t_{10}\}$.

Even though computing $NSky_{q.\mathcal{R}}$ requires to compute as many queries as the number of orders in $q.\mathcal{R}$, in the next section we show that these queries are actually easy to evaluate making the whole computation efficient.

3.1 Single Partial and Dynamic Dimension

In this section, we present an algorithm for computing $Sky_{q.\mathcal{R}}$. We consider a table T with $\mathcal{D} = \{A_1, \ldots, A_s, B\}$ where B is the unique partially and dynamically ordered dimension. Theorem 1 and its Corollary 1 suggest an algorithm for evaluating queries $Sky_{q.\mathcal{R}}$ on T: it evaluates sub-queries, i.e., the c-skyline by considering every $o \in q.\mathcal{R}$. The union of the sub-queries results is $NSky_{q.\mathcal{R}}$ and thus its complement to T is the response to $Sky_{q.\mathcal{R}}$.

The bottleneck of this direct implementation belongs to the multiple computations of $NSky_{\{o\}}$. Before presenting our solution, let us first make the following observation: Let o be an order, and let t be a tuple whose value in the dynamic dimension B is not mentioned in the preference $\{o\}$. Let $t' \in T$. Then

- $t \sqsubset_\mathcal{D} t' \Rightarrow t[B] = t'[B]$
- $t' \sqsubset_\mathcal{D} t \Rightarrow t[B] = t'[B]$

Said differently, and from the domination relationship, these tuples whose B value does not belong to o can be comparable to only those tuples sharing the same value on B. For example, consider the query q related to a *single-ton* preference $q.\mathcal{R} = \{(horror, thriller)\}$ stating that *horrors* are preferred to *thrillers* but there is no preference among the remaining genres. The tuples whose genre does not belong to the above two are comparable to only those with the same genre. Hence, we can partition them and restrict the comparisons to the so obtained subsets. To continue the example, we get the partition $\{\{t_1, t_8\}_c, \{t_2, t_9\}_s, \{t_5\}_r, \{t_6, t_{10}\}_a\}$. The first part $\{t_1, t_8\}_c$ corresponds to the tuples whose genre is $c(omedy)$. To this partition we can add a special part containing the remaining tuples, i.e., $\{t_3, t_4, t_7\}$. Now, each part can be processed independently to check whether a tuple is dominated or not. For example, comparing t_3 to t_5 is needless because they belong to different parts.

To summarize, computing the c-skyline wrt a *singleton* preference consists in partitioning the data into subsets of comparable tuples and identify those dominated within each subset. We formalize the above statement in Proposition 1, but first we define a dataset *part*.

Definition 5 (Part). *Given $\mathcal{D}$ and T. Let $D \in \mathcal{D}$. A part of T wrt a value d of D, denoted $\Pi_{[D|d]}(T)$, is the set $\{t \in T | t[D] = d\}$.*

Proposition 1. *Given $\mathcal{D} = \{A_1, \ldots, A_s, B\}$ and T. Let $b_i, b_j \in dom(B)$ and q such that $q.\mathcal{R} = \{(b_i, b_j)\}$.*
$$NSky_{\{(b_i, b_j)\}}(T) = NSky_{\{(b_i, b_j)\}}(\Pi_{[B|b_i]}(T) \cup \Pi_{[B|b_j]}(T)) \cup \bigcup_{\forall b_k \in dom(B)} NSky_{\{(b_i, b_j)\}}(\Pi_{[B|b_k]}(T)) \text{ where } b_k \neq b_i, b_j.$$

Example 5. Again, consider the movie dataset in Table 1. Let q be a skyline query s.t. $q.\mathcal{R} = \{(horror, thriller)\}$ then
$$NSky_{q.\mathcal{R}}(T) = NSky_{\{(h,t)\}}(\Pi_{[genre|h]}(T) \cup \Pi_{[genre|t]}(T)) \cup NSky_{\{(h,t)\}}(\Pi_{[genre|c]}(T)) \cup NSky_{\{(h,t)\}}(\Pi_{[genre|s]}(T)) \cup NSky_{\{(h,t)\}}(\Pi_{[genre|r]}(T)) \cup NSky_{\{(h,t)\}}(\Pi_{[genre|a]}(T)) = \{t_1, t_3, t_8, t_9, t_{10}\}$$

Algorithm dySky_1d. Algorithm 1 is the implementation of Proposition 1. First the variable $NSky$ which will store the dominated tuples is initialized (line 2). Then for each order $(b_i, b_j) \in q.\mathcal{R}$, the algorithm computes the c-skyline in two steps: (i) it computes P, the subset of tuples having the values b_i, b_j on dimension B, then computes dominated tuples in P (line 4–5). (ii) It iterates on all values $b_k \neq b_i, b_j$ of the domain of B, partitions T wrt to these values, and compute the dominated tuples within each partition (line 6–7). $Sky_{q.\mathcal{R}}$ is only $T \setminus NSky$.

Algorithm 1: dySky_1d

Input: a set of dimensions $\mathcal{D} = \{A_1, \ldots, A_s, B\}$, a dataset T, a query q
Output: $Sky_{q.\mathcal{R}}$

1 **begin**
2 $\quad NSky \leftarrow \emptyset$
3 $\quad$ **foreach** $(b_i, b_j) \in q.\mathcal{R}$ **in parallel do**
4 $\quad\quad P \leftarrow \Pi_{[B|b_i]}(T) \cup \Pi_{[B|b_j]}(T)$
5 $\quad\quad NSky \leftarrow NSky \cup NSky_{\{(b_i,b_j)\}}(P)$
6 $\quad\quad$ **foreach** $(b_k) \in dom(B) \setminus \{b_i, b_j\}$ **do**
7 $\quad\quad\quad NSky \leftarrow NSky \cup NSky_{\{(b_i,b_j)\}}(\Pi_{[B|b_k]}(T))$

8 **return** $T \setminus NSky$

Complexity Analysis. First, we consider the time complexity for evaluating a skyline query wrt some dataset of size v and over c dimensions as $O(v^2 \cdot c)$. Likewise the time complexity for evaluating the complementary skyline. Now, regarding our algorithm, let $n = |T|$ be the size of the dataset T, $s + 1$ be the number of its dimensions and m be the number of values in $dom(B)$. Consider that the values in $dom(B)$ are uniformly distributed over T. Then the size of each part wrt B is $v = \frac{n}{m}$. Let q be a query. The algorithm iterates on all orders in $q.\mathcal{R}$, hence $|q.\mathcal{R}|$ iterations. For every (b_i, b_j) in $q.\mathcal{R}$, (i) it partitions and computes the c-skyline wrt every value in $dom(B)$, hence $O(m \cdot (\frac{n}{m})^2 \cdot s)$, and (ii) it partitions and computes the c-skyline wrt values b_i and b_j, hence $O((2\frac{n}{m})^2 \cdot s)$. The overall time complexity is then $O(|q.\mathcal{R}| \cdot (\frac{n}{m})^2 \cdot s)$. Regarding space complexity, $dySky_1d$ maintains a solution set which size is up to input size n.

In the next sections, we highlight two properties that we implement in Algorithm 2, an optimized version of Algorithm 1.

The Extended Preference. Observe in Algorithm 1 (lines 6–7) that for every order (b_i, b_j), we compute a non skyline set for every $b_k \notin \{b_i, b_j\}$. According to this observation, we modify our algorithm so that every b_k not appearing in any order of a query is processed only once. We achieve this by extending the input preferences as follows:

Definition 6 (Extended Preference). *Let $\mathcal{R}$ be a preference on dimension B. Let $U(\mathcal{R})$ denotes the values in $dom(B)$ not mentioned in $\mathcal{R}$. The extended preference $\hat{\mathcal{R}}$ is $\mathcal{R} \cup \{(b_i, b_i)|\forall b_i \in U(\mathcal{R})\}$.*

Intuitively, adding these "artificial" orders forces Algorithm 1 to compare the tuples sharing a same value not mentioned in a preference $\mathcal{R}$. Therefore, the nested loop in Lines 6–7 can now be completely removed from that Algorithm since the outerloop (line 3) already handles those values b_k, provided that as input we have an extended preference. In the following, we consider that all preferences are extended.

Incrementally Discarding Dominated Tuples. Observe that given two orders $o_1 \; o_2$,

$$NSky_{\{o_1\}}(T) \cup NSky_{\{o_2\}}(T) = NSky_{\{o_1\}}(T \setminus NSky_{\{o_2\}}(T))$$

The tuples which do not belong to the skyline wrt order o_2, i.e. $NSky_{\{o_2\}}(T)$, should not be reconsidered for computing $NSky_{\{o_1\}}$.

We implement Algorithm 2 according to the above properties. The complexity of

---

Algorithm 2: dySky_1d_optimized

Input: a set of dimensions $\mathcal{D} = \{A_1, \ldots, A_s, B\}$, a dataset T, a query q
Output: $Sky_{q.\mathcal{R}}$

1 **begin**
2     $Sky \leftarrow T$
3   **foreach** $(b_i, b_j) \in q.\mathcal{R}$ *in parallel* **do**
4        $P \leftarrow \Pi_{[B|b_i]}(Sky) \cup \Pi_{[B|b_j]}(Sky)$
5        $Sky \leftarrow Sky \setminus NSky_{\{(b_i, b_j)\}}(P)$

6 **return** Sky

Algorithm 2 remains the same as that of Algorithm 1, however in practice, these modifications show enhancement in performance.

Remark 2. One may observe that Sky is shared between concurrent processes. In practice, we implement Sky as a vector of Boolean of size T. An item is set to False if the underlying tuple is found dominated.

3.2 Multiple Partial and Dynamic Dimensions

In this section, we present our approach for datasets with partially and dynamically ordered dimensions, i.e. $\mathcal{D} = \{A_1, \ldots, A_s, B_1, \ldots, B_l\}$. We recall that in this case, the preference $\mathcal{R}$ is composed of preferences over every dimension, i.e. $\mathcal{R} = \{R_1, \ldots, R_l\}$. Corollary 2 is a consequence of Theorem 1 when considering multiple partially ordered dimensions.

Corollary 2. *Given* $\mathcal{D} = \{A_1, \ldots, A_s, B_1, \ldots, B_l\}$, *a dataset* T, *and a query* q *such that* $q.\mathcal{R} = \{R_1, \ldots, R_l\}$. *Let* $t \in T$, *then* $t \notin Sky_{q.\mathcal{R}}$ *iff* $\exists(o_1, \ldots, o_l) \in R_1 \times \cdots \times R_l$ *s.t.* $t \notin Sky_{\{(o_1, \ldots, o_l)\}}$.

As said in Sect. 3.1, an algorithm which naively computes $Sky_{\{(o_1, \ldots, o_l)\}} \forall (o_1, \ldots, o_l) \in R_1 \times \cdots \times R_l$ does not take advantage of skyline properties. Firstly and for the ease of the presentation, we detail our approach in case of two partially ordered dimensions, then we generalize to the case of l partially ordered dimensions. Consider the dataset and the preference $\mathcal{R}$ depicted respectively in Tables 3 and 4. Note that smaller values are preferred. Likewise the case of one partially

Table 3. Dataset with two dynamic dimensions

	A_1	A_2	A_3	B_1	B_2
t_1	1	0	1	b_{11}	b_{21}
t_2	0	0	1	b_{11}	b_{22}
t_3	1	1	1	b_{11}	b_{21}
t_4	1	2	1	b_{13}	b_{21}
t_5	1	0	2	b_{12}	b_{23}

Table 4. The preference $q.\mathcal{R}$

R_1	R_2
$o_{11} = (b_{11}, b_{12})$	$o_{21} = (b_{21}, b_{22})$
$o_{12} = (b_{11}, b_{13})$	$o_{22} = (b_{22}, b_{23})$
	$o_{23} = (b_{21}, b_{23})$

ordered dimension, our approach consists in computing the sets of comparable tuples T wrt the preference $q.\mathcal{R}$ and then deduce the dominated tuples. To that purpose, we proceed as follows: (i) we compute the subsets of tuples T_1 and T_2 having respectively values in o_{11} and o_{12}, i.e., the orders belonging to the preference related to the first dimension B_1, (ii) from T_1 and T_2, we compute the subsets of tuples having respectively values in o_{21}, o_{22} and o_{23}, i.e., the orders in the preference over dimension B_2. We illustrate this process in Fig. 2. Let $\mathcal{T}$ be the set of the so computed subsets. Then a tuple t belongs to the skyline wrt T iff it does not belong to any complementary skyline of $T' \forall T' \in \mathcal{T}$. For example, in Fig. 2, the c-skyline of the subset in the left most leaf is $\{t_3, t_4\}$, hence, $t_3, t_4 \notin Sky_{q.\mathcal{R}}$. One may verify that the union of the c-skylines is $\{t_3, t_4, t_5\}$ and therefore, $Sky_{q.\mathcal{R}} = T \setminus \{t_3, t_4, t_5\}$.

We formalize and generalize the above explanation in the following result.

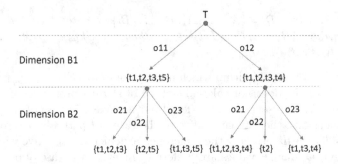

Fig. 2. Processing q

Proposition 2. *Given* $\mathcal{D}$, T, *and a query* q *such that* $q.\mathcal{R} = \{R_1, \ldots, R_l\}$. *Let* $\mathcal{O} = R_1 \times \cdots \times R_l$. *Then*

$$NSky_{q.\mathcal{R}}(T) = \bigcup_{o \in \mathcal{O}} NSky_{\{o\}}\left(\bigcap_{i=1}^{l} \Pi_{[B_i | b_e \vee b_f \ s.t. \ b_e, b_f \in o_i]}\right)$$

Intuitively, the above proposition simply states that by computing the dominated tuples in each obtained subset, we get the set of all dominated tuples. Hence, the skyline set.

Remark 3. One may notice that the obtained subsets do not form a partition. For example, the right most sub-tree in Fig. 2, we have two sets containing t_1, t_3 and t_4. This means that these tuples are compared twice and each time, t_3 and t_4 are found dominated by t_1. To avoid this redundant computation, it suffices to remove the dominated tuples from the underlying data as soon as possible. So, the right most subset will actually contain only t_1.

Now we present how we translate Proposition 2 to a concrete algorithm.

Algorithm dySky_md. The algorithm takes as input T and a query q, and returns $Sky_{q.\mathcal{R}}$. It is composed of a main routine and a recursive procedure called *recursiveNSky*. The variable $NSky$ stores the complementary skyline throughout the process. It is initialized by an empty set. The variable i indicates the dimension the algorithm is currently processing. In the beginning, i is set to 1, hence the process starts with dimension B_1. The algorithm calls the procedure *recursiveNSky* with the arguments: (i) i, i.e. which indicates the first dimension, (ii) the dataset T and (iii) $NSky$ (line 4). Regarding the procedure *recursiveNSky*, for each order o in R_i, it filters T' wrt o (line 3), then if $i < l$, i.e. the algorithm is not processing the last dimension, it recalls *recursiveNSky* with new parameters(line 5). Otherwise $(i = l)$, i.e. the algorithm is currently processing the last dimension B_l, it computes the complementary skyline wrt T'' and add it to $NSky$ (line 7). Finally, the skyline wrt the query q is T minus $NSky$ (line 5 in the main routine).

Algorithm 3: dySky_md

Input: a set of dimensions $D = \{D_1, \ldots, D_s, B_1, \ldots, B_l\}$, a dataset $T(D)$, a query q

Output: $Sky_{q.\mathcal{R}}(T)$

1 **Procedure** $recursiveNSky(i, T', NSky)$

2   **foreach** $o \in R_i$ **in parallel do**

3      $T'' \leftarrow \Pi_{[B_i|o.left]}(T') \cup \Pi_{[B_i|o.right]}(T')$

4   **if** $i < l$ **then**

5        $recursiveNSky(i+1, T'', NSky)$

6   **else**

7        $NSky \leftarrow NSky \cup NSky(T'')$

1 **begin**

2    $NSky \leftarrow \emptyset$

3    $i \leftarrow 1$

4    $recursiveNSky(i, T, NSky)$

5 **return** $T \setminus NSky$

Complexity Analysis. Given the parameters m, l, n and s. Suppose the preferences on the dynamic dimensions have the same number of orders r, i.e., $|R_i| = r, \forall i \in [1..l]$. At each level, *dySky_md* iterates on r orders. Globally, the algorithm iterates r^l times. We consider the filtering operations take a constant time. The argument here is that one can use bitmap indexes on the B_i's dimensions. The final step consists in computing the complementary skyline. In case of uniform distribution of the values in $dom(B_i) \forall i \in [1..l]$, at the last level of filtering, the datasets T' contains $\frac{n}{m^l}$ tuples. Then the overall complexity is $O(r^l * (\frac{n}{m^l})^2 * (s + l))$. When the preferences R_i's are total, r equals $\frac{m(m-1)}{2}$. In such case, this algorithm's complexity becomes that of a naive algorithm, however, in practice *dySky_md* performs better.

4 Optimization Using Materialization

As we have seen so far, the main idea of *dySky* algorithm is to take a query q and decompose it into a set of sub-queries q_i. Each of them operates on a subset of T obtained by a sequence of filters. For example, let us consider again query q (see Table 4) from the previous section. In order to answer q, we compute 6 complementary skylines, i.e. 6 sub-queries, as illustrated in Fig. 2. Consider the left most subset in that Figure which is obtained by the filter sequence $((b_{11}, b_{12}), (b_{21}, b_{22}))$. Consider the sub-query q_1 which computes the complementary skyline regarding this subset. Suppose now that the answer of q_1 is materialized. Then whenever q is issued, we get the answer of q_1 automatically. Likewise, the queries sharing the same sub-query q_1 are optimized thanks to this materialization. Obviously, by materializing all possible sub-queries, we optimize all possible queries. This solution is practical only for cases where the number of possible sub-queries is reasonable. When this number is too large, a pragmatic solution is to materialize a subset of these sub-queries. The choice of the best subset should be driven by a query workload. This is the problem we address in this section.

Firstly, we give some definitions needed for this section. Then we address the full materialization of the sub-queries, i.e. we consider that there is no limitation on memory space and we materialize all possible sub-queries. Later, we consider the case where memory space is restricted, and we address the partial materialization of the sub-queries, i.e., we materialize a set of sub-queries under space constraint.

4.1   Materialization Structure

Each sub-query q_i is uniquely identified by a filtering sequence seq_i. Before defining a sequence, we firstly define the set of orders wrt a dimension B_i.

Definition 7. *Given a partially ordered dimension B_i. $Orders(B_i) = \{(b_{ij}, b_{ik}) \in dom(B_i) \times dom(B_i)\}$ is the set of all possible orders wrt B_i.*

It is easy to see that $|Orders(B_i)| = |dom(B_i)|^2$. Given a set of partially ordered dimensions $\mathcal{B} = \{B_1, \ldots, B_l\}$, a sequence is an *l-tuple* which belongs to the Cartesian product $Orders(B_1) \times \cdots \times Orders(B_l)$. Formally speaking,

Definition 8 (Sequence). *Given $\mathcal{B} = \{B_1, \ldots, B_l\}$. A sequence is an element of $Orders(B_1) \times \cdots \times Orders(B_l)$. Consequently, the set of all possible sequences is $\Sigma(\mathcal{B}) = \{seq | seq \in Orders(B_1) \times \cdots \times Orders(B_l)\}$.*

Clearly, $|\Sigma(\mathcal{B})| = \Pi_{i=1}^{l} |Orders(B_i)|$. Hereafter, we note just Σ when $\mathcal{B}$ is understood.

Example 6. Consider again Table 3. We have $dom(B_1) = \{b_{11}, b_{12}, b_{13}\}$ and $dom(B_2) = \{b_{21}, b_{22}, b_{23}\}$. One possible sequence is $((b_{13}, b_{11}), (b_{22}, b_{22}))$. Σ contains in total 81 sequences.

The sub-queries materialization structure is a set of pairs (seq_i, CS_i) such that seq_i is the filtering sequence related to a query q_i and CS_i is the complementary skyline wrt the filtered data.

Definition 9 (seqStruct). *Given $\mathcal{D} = \{A_1, \ldots, A_s, B_1, \ldots, B_l\}$ and T. $seqStruct = \{(seq_i, CS_i) | seq_i \in \Sigma$ and $CS_i \subseteq T\}$.*

Finally, given a query q, $sequences(q)$ is the set of sequences related to q. Formally speaking,

Definition 10 (Sequences related to a query).
Given $\{B_1, \ldots, B_l\}$ and a query q such that $q.\mathcal{R} = \{R_1, \ldots, R_l\}$.

$$sequences(q) = \{seq \in R_1 \times \cdots \times R_l\}$$

Example 7. Consider $q.\mathcal{R}$ depicted in Table 4. It has 6 related sequences. E.g., (o_{11}, o_{21}) and (o_{11}, o_{22}).

4.2   Full Materialization

In a nutshell, the process to materialize all possible sub-queries is to iterate on all possible sequences seq_i in Σ, to filter data wrt seq_i and to compute the complementary skyline to be stored in $seqStruct$ $\mathcal{F}$. Algorithm 4 ($dySkySeq\_build$) designed to this aim proceeds in a smarter way. Intuitively, one may observe that each sequence is actually a conjunction of conditions and several conditions may share the same conjunct prefix. For example, the sequences (o_{11}, o_{21}) and (o_{11}, o_{22}) share the same prefix o_{11}. To filter T wrt these two sequences, we first consider o_{11}. The result is then used for both o_{21} and o_{22}.

Algorithm dySkySeq_build. This procedure (see Algorithm 4) takes $\mathcal{D}$ and T as input, and returns a $seqStruct$ $\mathcal{F}$. At the beginning, $\mathcal{F}$ is empty. Variable i indicates the dimension the algorithm is processing and is initialized to 1. Variable seq is a stack structure and is used to store the sequences. The algorithm proceeds in a Depth-First fashion. It calls the recursive function $recursiveSeq$ with parameters (i) i to indicate the dimension B_i, (ii) T, (iii) seq, and (iv) the set $\mathcal{F}$ (line 5). Inside $recursiveSeq$, T' is filtered wrt B_i and o is pushed onto seq (line 3–4). If $(i < l)$, i.e. , the algorithm is not processing the last dimension, it recalls $recursiveSeq$ with new parameters (line 6). Otherwise, i.e. $(i = l)$, at this step, seq contains l orders. Hence it computes the complementary skyline wrt T'' and inserts the pair $(seq, NSky_{\{seq\}}(T''))$ in $\mathcal{F}$ (line 8). Finally, o is popped from the sequence (line 9).

Query Answering. We describe here how to evaluate a query using $\mathcal{F}$. Algorithm 5 ($dySkySeq\_qa$) takes as input $\mathcal{F}$, T, and a query q and returns $Sky_{q.\mathcal{R}}$. The algorithm simply merges the complementary skylines associated to sequences related to the query q.

4.3   Constrained Materialization

Generally, materializing all the sub-queries can be costly. In this section we address partial materialization of the sub-queries, i.e., we materialize only a subset $\mathcal{P} \subseteq \mathcal{F}$. However, we want to select the sequences in $\mathcal{P}$ such that the answering cost of a workload $\mathcal{Q}$ is optimal. Without any constraint, the solution to this problem is obvious: materialize all and only the sequences related to $\mathcal{Q}$. Even when considering just $\mathcal{Q}$ and not all possible queries, the storage space may become prohibitive. So, we constrain the query cost optimization problem with an available memory storage H that has not to be overtaken by the chosen sequences to be materialized.

We start by defining the costs of answering queries and workloads. Then we present the partial materialization problem.

Query Answering Cost. We set the answering cost of a query q as the number of sequences related to q, namely,

$$Cost(q) = |sequences(q)|$$

Algorithm 4: dySkySeq_build

Input: a set of dimensions $\mathcal{D} = \{A_1, \ldots, A_s, B_1, \ldots, B_l\}$, a dataset T
Output: seqStruct $\mathcal{F}$
1 **Procedure** recursiveSeq($i, T', seq, \mathcal{F}$)
2　　**foreach** $o \in Orders(B_i)$ ***in parallel*** **do**
3　　　　$T'' \leftarrow \Pi_{[B_i|o.left]}(T') \cup \overline{\Pi_{[B_i|o.right]}(T')}$
4　　　　$seq.push(o)$
5　　　　**if** $i < l$ **then**
6　　　　　　$recursiveSeq(i+1, T'', seq, \mathcal{F})$
7　　　　**else**
8　　　　　　$\mathcal{F} \leftarrow \mathcal{F} \cup (seq, NSky_{\{seq\}}(T''))$
9　　　　$seq.pop(o)$

1 **begin**
2　　$\mathcal{F} \leftarrow \emptyset$
3　　$i \leftarrow 1$
4　　$seq \leftarrow \emptyset$
5　　$recursiveSeq(i, T, seq, \mathcal{F})$
6 **return** $\mathcal{V}$

Algorithm 5: dySkySeq_qa

Input: a query q, $\mathcal{F}$, T
Output: $Sky_{q.\mathcal{R}}$
1 **begin**
2　　$NSky \leftarrow \emptyset$
3　　**foreach** $seq \in sequences(q)$ **do**
4　　　　$NSky \leftarrow NSky \cup \mathcal{F}[seq]$
5 **return** $T \setminus NSky$

The rationale behind this choice of cost function is that, under uniform distribution, the size of the filtered data from which the complementary skyline is computed is the same whatever is the sequence.

Now consider a set of materialized sub-queries $\mathcal{P}$, then the cost of answering q through $\mathcal{P}$ is

$$Cost(q, \mathcal{P}) = Cost(q) - |\{p \in \mathcal{P}|p.seq \in sequences(q)\}|$$

In other words, partial materialization saves query execution time proportionally to the number of sub-queries that are already materialized. The cost of a workload $\mathcal{Q}$ wrt $\mathcal{P}$ is defined accordingly:

$$Cost(\mathcal{Q}, \mathcal{P}) = \sum_{q \in \mathcal{Q}} Cost(q, \mathcal{P})$$

Note that with the above definitions, when using full materialization, the cost of any query is null, thus $Cost(Q, \mathcal{F}) = 0$. This reflects the fact that retrieving a query answer is done without any effort.

In the next section, we formalize the problem of partial materialization of sub-queries, and we provide an algorithm to select the set $\mathcal{P}$.

Sequence Selection Problem. As said previously, the obvious way to optimize a workload Q is to cache the results of the sub-queries related to Q. Storing all these results may require a storage space larger than the available one H. So, one needs to select a subset fitting H.

Remark 4. Given a *seqStruct* $\mathcal{M}$, the required space to store $\mathcal{M}$, noted $res(\mathcal{M})$, is the total required space for storing complementary skylines related to sequences in $\mathcal{M}$.

The sequence selection problem we address is,

> **Problem SS** Given $\mathcal{D}$, T, a workload Q, a *seqStruct* S related to Q, and an integer $H \geq 0$, compute a set $\mathcal{M} \subseteq S$ such that $res(\mathcal{M}) \leq H$ and $Cost(Q, \mathcal{M})$ is minimum.

Unsurprisingly, problem **SS** is hard. This can be shown by considering a decision counterpart **VS** of **SS** and prove that it is NP-Complete. **VS** problem consists in checking whether there exists a solution of **SS** whose corresponding cost is less than some k.

Theorem 2. VS *problem is NP-Complete*

Proof. (Sketch) This can be done using a reduction of an instance of the Knapsack problem where the capacity W represents the input size.

Problem **SS** can be solved exactly by a 0-1 Integer Linear Program stated as follows:

$$\text{maximize} \sum_{j=1}^{n} g_j x_j$$
$$\text{subject to} \sum_{j=1}^{n} w_j x_j \leq W, \tag{1}$$
$$x_j \in \{0, 1\}, j = 1, \ldots, n$$

We set n as the size of S and W as H. The weight vector $(w_1, \ldots, w_n)$ equals $(|p_1.CS|, \ldots, |p_n.CS|) \forall p_i \in S$. The gain g_i represents the number of queries in Q which have the sequence $p_i.seq$ in their respective set of sequences. It is defined by the following formula.

$$g_i = Gain(p_i, \mathcal{Q}) = |\{q \in \mathcal{Q}|p_i.seq \in sequences(q)\}|$$

It is well known that 0-1 linear programs can be solved by dynamic programming techniques (e.g., see [10]). Since it is now standard and due to space limitation, we do not present this adapted algorithm to our setting. We just recall its precise complexity which is $O(|\mathcal{S}| * H)$.

In the present setting, i.e., partial materialization, when a query is submitted, it is first decomposed into a set of sub-queries. Some of them can be already materialized, thus their result is already available. The others are evaluated from scratch. The Algorithm 6 *dySkySeq_hybrid* implements this procedure.

Algorithm 6: dySkySeq_hybrid

Input: a query q, a *seqStruct* $\mathcal{M}$ and a dataset T

Output: $Sky_{q.\mathcal{R}}$

1 **Procedure** $computeSeq(i, T', seq, NSky)$
2      $T'' \leftarrow \Pi_{[B_i|seq[i].left]}(T') \cup \Pi_{[B_i|seq[i].right]}(T')$
3   **if** $i < l$ **then**
4         $computeSeq(i + 1, T'', seq, NSky)$
5   **else**
6         $NSky \leftarrow NSky \cup NSky_{\{seq\}}(T'')$

1 **begin**
2      $NSky \leftarrow \emptyset$
3   **foreach** $seq \in sequences(q)$ **do**
4   **if** $seq \in \mathcal{M}$ **then**
5            $NSky \leftarrow NSky \cup \mathcal{M}[seq]$
6   **else**
7            $computeSeq(1, T, seq, NSky)$
8 **return** $T \setminus NSky$

---

5   Related Work

We identify two main lines of previous works related to ours: (i) solutions targeting totally ordered data either sequentially or in parallel, and (ii) those addressing the case of dynamic partial orders.

5.1   Techniques for Totally Ordered Data

Since the introduction of the *skyline* operator by [5], several sequential algorithms have been proposed in the literature. Some are sort based, e.g., [3,7–9] and others are based on partitioning , e.g., [13–16]. To our knowledge, *BSkyTree* proposed in [14] is the state of the art sequential algorithm for totally ordered domains. As for parallel algorithms, they proceed by data partitioning either vertically (e.g., [2]) or horizontally (e.g., [1]). Note however that the optimization techniques used either for sequential or parallel solutions cannot be extended easily to partially ordered domains.

5.2 Techniques for Data with Dynamic Partial Orders

On the Fly Algorithms. In lattice theory, it is well known that every partial order can be embedded into a product of a set of total orders [4, 18]. This inspired [20] to propose CPS which consists in transforming each partially ordered dimension by a set of totally ordered ones then apply a classical algorithm. Because finding the minimal number of total orders is NP-complete, [20] used an approximate algorithm. [6] proposed to transform each partially ordered dimension into *two* totally ordered dimensions. The transformed dataset is then processed by any standard algorithm. However, the output may include false positives, because of the restricted number of total orders. So a filtering pass on the output is required. [17] proposed TSS a framework that transforms a partially ordered dimension into a *single* totally ordered dimension corresponding to one of its corresponding topological orders. Like [6], a filtering step is needed after getting a first skyline because of false negatives. Empirical studies showed that CPS combined to $BSkyTree$ outperforms techniques in [6, 17, 20]. So we retain this solution to compare it with ours, c.f Sect. 6.

Materialization Based Techniques. [11, 12, 19] addressed skyline queries when some dimensions are partially and dynamically ordered using materialization techniques. [19] proposed a tree-like structure *Ordered Skyline Tree OST* in order to materialize the skylines wrt every total preference. A query q related to a preference $q.\mathcal{R}$ is evaluated by combining the skylines of different total preferences. The memory usage of this tree can rapidly become a bottleneck because of the factorial number of total preferences. The authors proposed CST, a compressed version of OST but whose worst case memory usage is that of OST.

In [11] and its extension [12], the authors proposed answering queries through cached queries by a refinement process. Let q, q' be two queries and $q.\mathcal{R}, q'.\mathcal{R}$ be their respective preferences. q is a *refinement* of q' iff $q'.\mathcal{R} \subseteq q.\mathcal{R}$. In such case it is easy to see that $Sky_{q.\mathcal{R}} \subseteq Sky_{q'.\mathcal{R}}$. Suppose that a set Q of queries is cached and consider q as a new submitted query. Their solution consists first to find a refinement $q' \in Q$ of q and then use q' result to evaluate q. The authors propose an index structure to find a refinement given a query. Unfortunately, this index is not complete in that, some refinements can be missed.

6   Experiments

In this section we compare our proposals to relevant literature techniques. We consider both non materialization and materialization based solutions. For the first family, we consider the algorithm *CPS* proposed by [20] as a representative solution. We recall that *CPS* transforms partially ordered dimensions into totally ordered dimensions. We combine it with *BSkyTree* [14] in order to compute the skyline over the transformed dataset. For materialization-based techniques, we consider *Ordered Skyline Tree (OST)* structure [19]. In the remainder, we denote by *OST* both the structure and its corresponding algorithm for answering queries. Moreover we consider the query answering through refinement technique as presented in [11,12] and we denote it by *Ref*. We adapted the *BSkyTree* algorithm and its authors implementation so that it returns the complementary skyline which is the main procedure of our solutions.

The experiments are organized in three parts:

1. In Sect. 6.1 and regarding query answering time, we evaluate algorithms which answer queries on the fly, i.e., *dySky_md* and *CPS* as well as those using precomputed structures, i.e., *dySkySeq_qa* and *OST*.
2. In Sect. 6.2 and for pre-computation based techniques, we compare their respective structure build time and their memory consumption.
3. We show the ability of *dySky* to compete with the refinement strategy *Ref* proposed in [11,12]. We consider the case where a set of queries is cached, and we measure the answering time of another set of queries by both techniques. Refer to Sect. 6.3.
4. Finally, we evaluate other specific aspects of *dySky* in Sect. 6.4. Specifically, we assess the linear cost function of answering queries presented in Sect. 4.3. We evaluate the impact of partial materialization of sub-queries on the query answering performance, and we evaluate the impact of multithreading on *dySky*.

Hardware and Software. Experiments are conducted on a machine equipped with 96 cores cadenced with a frequency up to 3.4 Ghz, 1 TB RAM and running CentOS linux. Regarding software, we use *BSkyTree* authors version. We did our best effort to implement reliably *CPS*, *OST* and *Ref* as they are not publicly available. Software is in c++ and available on GitHub[3].

Datasets. We use both synthetic and real datasets commonly used in benchmarking skyline solutions. Synthetic datasets are generated through the framework [5] with independent (INDE) and anti-correlated (ANTI) distribution. Both datasets are initially composed of totally and statically ordered dimensions. We augment them with nominal dimensions where the values are uniformly distributed.

Table 5 shows the different parameters for synthetic data. Bold values are the default.

Table 6 shows the characteristics of the real data in addition to their respective skyline size wrt the totally ordered dimensions.

Due to space limitation, we do not show experiments with different values of s for generated datasets. Nonetheless this parameter is the less relevant to compare the techniques.

---

[3] https://github.com/karimalami7/dySky.

Table 5. Synthetic datasets

Parameter	Values
n (dataset size)	$100K, \mathbf{1M}, 10M$
s (static dims)	**6**
l (dynamic dims)	$1, \mathbf{2}, 3$
m (dynamic dims values)	$10, \mathbf{15}, 20$
distribution	**ANTI**, INDE

Table 6. Real datasets

Parameter	POKER	IPUMS	HOUSE
n	1M	75836	127931
s	11	10	6
l	2	2	3
m	15	30	10
$|Skyline|$	14131	3852	127931

Queries Generation. In some of the following experiments we need to generate random queries. These are completely defined by their respective preferences on the B_i's attributes. Each preference on a dimension B_i is actually a DAG whose set of nodes is $dom(B_i)$. Thus, we generate random DAGs on $dom(B_i)$ following a *density* parameter $\rho \in [0,1]$. Let's recall its definition. Let $G = (V, E)$ be a DAG, then the density of G is $\rho(G) = \dfrac{2|E|}{|V| * (|V| - 1)}$. That's, the denser is G the more the values in $dom(B_i)$ are comparable. By default, we set $\rho = 0.5$.

6.1   Query Answering Time

Here we compare our solutions to its competitors in terms of query answering time. In each case, we execute a same workload of 50 queries and we report the average execution time of all solutions. Sometimes OST values are not reported either because its related structure saturated the available memory or its execution did not terminate in a reasonable time (>24 h).

Varying n, m, l and Data Distribution. Figures. 3, 4 and 5 depict the results with respectively 1, 2 and 3 dynamic dimensions. A first observation is that OST fails to build its structure in many configurations. When its structure can be built, the query answering time of OST is close to non materialization-based approaches CPS and $dySky\_md$ (see Fig. 3). Regarding CPS, we observe that $dySkySeq\_qa$ and $dySky\_md$ perform better with (i) larger and/or (ii) anti-correlated datasets, i.e., the harder cases. For example, in Figs. 3, 4 and 5, for $n = 1M$, $dySky\_md$ and $dySkySeq\_qa$ are respectively about one and three orders of magnitude faster than CPS.

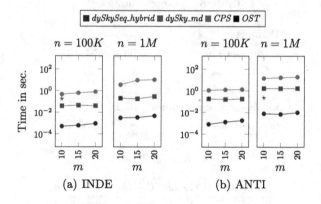

Fig. 3. Query answering with $l = 1$

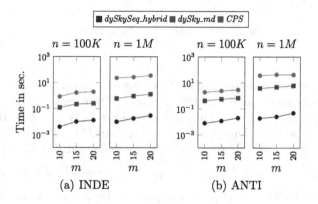

Fig. 4. Query answering time with $l = 2$

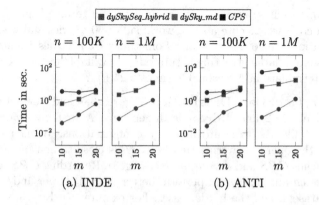

Fig. 5. Query answering time with $l = 3$

Figure 6 depicts the query answering times for a dataset of $10M$ tuples and by varying both l and m. Globally, we can see that both $dySkySeq\_qa$ and $dySky\_md$ have better performances than CPS, however $dySkySeq\_qa$ scales less good than the two other solutions well wrt l. This trend suggests that materialization would be of no great added value with higher values of l, say $l \geq 6$.

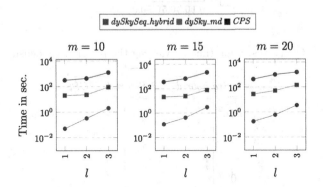

Fig. 6. Query answering time with $10M$ tuples

Varying the Preferences Density ρ. We generate queries whose $\rho \in \{0.1, 0.3, 0.5, 0.7, 0.9\}$. Figure 7 depicts the results with a dataset having the default parameters. We see in the results that for a low density, $dySky$ outperforms CPS by nearly two orders of magnitude. The gap tends to become smaller as the density grows. Recall that the lower the density, the lower the number of orders, while for CPS, the lower the density, the higher the number of dimensions in the transformed dataset.

Querying Real Data. Figure 8 shows the obtained results. These confirm the previous findings, i.e., $dySky$ with its two versions, clearly outperforms CPS.

6.2   Precomputation Time and Storage

In this section we compare the precomputation time and storage of both $\mathcal{F}$ and OST structure related respectively to $dySkySeq\_qa$ and OST algorithms. We recall that $dySky\_md$ and CPS does not require precomputation and their space complexity is linear to the size of the input. Regarding precomputation time, for $\mathcal{F}$ we measure the execution time of Algorithm 4 $dySkySeq\_build$ and for OST we measure the time of building the whole tree. W.r.t storage, we count the total number of tuples stored by each technique. Figure 9 depicts the obtained results with a dataset having one partially ordered dimension. We see that OST can not terminate when $m > 10$. When $m = 10$, the gap is large between OST and $dySky$ wrt both time and storage. Results wrt datasets having more than one

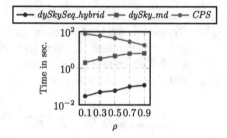

Fig. 7. Query answering time by varying the preference's density ρ

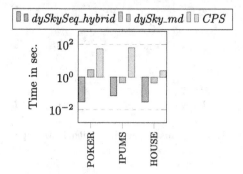

Fig. 8. Query answering time with real data

dynamic order are not reported as OST did not terminate for any configuration. This is due to the high size of the tree when both l and m grow as explained in Sect. 5.

6.3   Caching Queries

In this experiment we show the ability of $dySky$ to compete with the refinement strategy proposed in [11,12] to optimize the queries via caching. To this aim, we consider the following scenario: Firstly, a set of queries Q_1 is selected randomly and its result is cached. Recall that for a query $q \in Q_1$ $dySky$ caches the results of sub-queries related to q while Ref caches the result of q. Then a second set Q_2 of queries is evaluated using the previously cached results. Regarding Ref, a query $q \in Q$ can benefit from the cache iff there exists q' in the cache which is a refinement of q while following $dySky$, q benefits from the cache if at least one of its sub-queries is cached. We conducted experiments by varying the size of Q_1. We set $n = 100K$, $m = 10$ and $l = 2$, and a set Q_2 of 50 queries. Figure 10 reports the average execution time of queries in Q_2. As it may be observed, in all cases $dySky$ provides better execution times than Ref making it a serious candidate to be used in a caching context. More precisely, Fig. 10 shows that query answering time of Ref does not improve considerably when caching more queries. While $dySky\_hybrid$ performance improves until $|Q_1| = 100$ then it

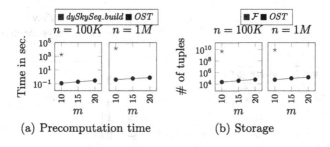

Fig. 9. Precomputation with one dynamic dimension

remains almost constant with larger $|Q_1|$. This is explained by the fact that the maximum number of distinct sub-queries ($m^{2l} = 10^4$) can be reached with few queries. Figure 10 suggests that with $|Q_1| = 100$, the number of distinct subqueries becomes close to 10^4, i.e., all queries in Q_2 are completely optimized. However, for *Ref* technique, even with a workload of 1000 queries, a refinement is hardly found for queries in Q_2.

6.4 Evaluating Other Aspects of DySky

In this section, we evaluate specific aspects of *dySky*.

Query Answering Cost Estimation. In Sect. 4.3, we have set the cost of answering a query q to be the number of sequences related to q. In this experiment, we want to confirm this supposition. To that purpose, we evaluate a set of queries each having a different number of sequences. For this experiment, we consider a dataset with $n = 100K$, $l = 2$ and $m = 10$. We generate 6 queries having respectively 60, 120, 240, 480, 960 and 1920 related sequences. The blue curve in Fig. 11 depicts the obtained results, and the red curve is used to show the linear trend. We can see that the curves overlap, hence, the cost of answering a query q is clearly linear wrt its number of sequences $sequences(q)$.

Query Answering Time with Partial Materialization of the Sub-queries. We consider the following scenario: we want to optimize the answering of a workload Q. Let P be the *seqStruct* containing only sequences involved in Q and let M be the size of P. Obviously, if we store P, queries in Q are completely evaluated through materialized sub-queries. Now we consider the cases where the available memory size is equal to fractions of M, i.e. $\frac{M}{2}$, $\frac{M}{4}$, $\frac{M}{8}$ and $\frac{M}{16}$. In this experiment, we evaluate the query answering time of queries in Q by considering sets $M \subseteq P$ output of Problem SS presented in Sect. 4.3 wrt values M, $\frac{M}{2}$, $\frac{M}{4}$, $\frac{M}{8}$, and $\frac{M}{16}$ for H. We consider datasets with $n = 10M$, $l = 1$, and m in $\{10, 15, 20\}$ as well as a workload Q of 100 queries. Figure 12 depicts the results. We globally observe the same trend for all values of m. When H is equal to M, P is completely materialized and therefore queries in Q are fully

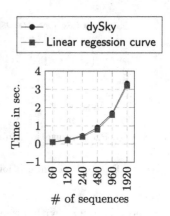

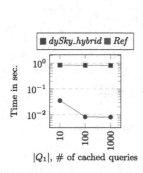

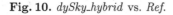

Fig. 10. *dySky_hybrid* vs. *Ref.*   **Fig. 11.** Query answering cost

optimized. As long as we reduce the available memory H, the query answering time grows as now some sub-queries need to be computed from scratch.

Parallel Processing Throughput of DySky. In this experiment, we want to measure the multithreadring performance of *dySky*. We specifically consider Algorithm 4 *dySkySeq_build*. We run experiments with parameters $n = 10M$, $s = 6$, $l = 2$ and $m = 20$. We vary the number of parallel threads in $\{6, 12, 24, 48, 96\}$. Figure 13 depicts the results. We use the red curve just to show the linear trend. The results show that our algorithm is highly parallelizable because the sequential part is negligeable.

6.5   Concluding Remarks

Globally, the performed experiments showed that our proposals outperform its competitors. Regarding query answering on the fly, we showed that in presence of challenging datasets, i.e., large and anti-correlated datasets, our algorithm *dySky_md* performs better than CPS which, to our knowledge, is the state of the art algorithm. Regarding precomputation based technique, we showed that our proposed structure, compared to OST, (i) is built faster, (ii) stores less data (iii) and provides better query answering performance. Regarding queries caching solutions, we showed that with much less cached queries, our proposal achieves better query performance than the refinement technique *Ref.* Finally, and thanks to *dySky* design, we showed that it is highly parallelizable.

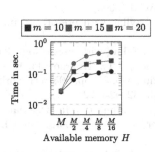

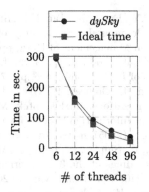

Fig. 12. Query answering with restricted memory

Fig. 13. Parallel throughput

7   Conclusion

In this paper we presented *dySky*, an approach for optimizing skyline queries over data with two kinds of dimensions: those that are totally and statically ordered and those that are partially and dynamically ordered. Given a query q and its related preference on the attributes domain $q.\mathcal{R}$, *dySky* decomposes q into a set of sub-queries q_i, each of which operates on a small part of the input data. This decomposition leads naturally to a parallel procedure. In a further step for optimization, we proposed the sub-queries results as a building block for materialization. In this context, we addressed both full and constrained partial materialization driven by a workload. The empirical experimental results we provide, show the superiority of *dySky* compared to its competitors. Particularly when the partial ordered domains have low cardinality. We believe that in practice, users are not willing to provide partial orders between a large number of values.

References

1. Afrati, F.N., Koutris, P., Suciu, D., Ullman, J.D.: Parallel skyline queries. Theory Comput. Syst. **57**(4), 1008–1037 (2015)
2. Balke, W.-T., Güntzer, U., Zheng, J.X.: Efficient distributed skylining for web information systems. In: Bertino, E., et al. (eds.) EDBT 2004. LNCS, vol. 2992, pp. 256–273. Springer, Heidelberg (2004). https://doi.org/10.1007/978-3-540-24741-8_16
3. Bartolini, I., Ciaccia, P., Patella, M.: Efficient sort-based skyline evaluation, **33**, 31 (2008)
4. Bernhard, K., Vygen, J.: Combinatorial Optimization: Theory and Algorithms, 3rd edn. Springer, Heidelberg (2005, 2008)
5. Börzsönyi, S., Kossmann, D., Stocker, K.: The skyline operator. In: Proceedings of ICDE Conference, pp. 421–430 (2001)

6. Chan, C.Y., Eng, P.K., Tan, K.L.: Stratified computation of skylines with partially-ordered domains. In: Proceedings of the 2005 ACM SIGMOD International Conference on Management of Data, pp. 203–214. ACM (2005)

7. Chomicki, J., Godfrey, P., Gryz, J., Liang, D.: Skyline with presorting. In: Proceedings of ICDE Conference, pp. 717–719 (2003)

8. Chomicki, J., Godfrey, P., Gryz, J., Liang, D.: Skyline with presorting: Theory and optimizations. In: Kłopotek, M.A., Wierzchoń, S.T., Trojanowski, K. (eds.) Intelligent Information Processing and Web Mining, vol. 31, pp. 595–604. Springer, Heidelberg (2005). https://doi.org/10.1007/3-540-32392-9_72

9. Godfrey, P., Shipley, R., Gryz, J.: Maximal vector computation in large data sets. In: Proceedings of the 31st International Conference on Very Large Data Bases, pp. 229–240. VLDB Endowment (2005)

10. Greenberg, H.: A dynamic programming solution to integer linear programs. J. Math. Anal. Appl. **26**(2), 454–459 (1969)

11. Hsueh, Y.-L., Hascoet, T.: Caching support for skyline query processing with partially ordered domains. IEEE Trans. Knowl. Data Eng. **26**(11), 2649–2661 (2014)

12. Hsueh, Y.-L., Lin, C.-C., Chang, C.-C.: An efficient indexing method for skyline computations with partially ordered domains. IEEE Trans. Knowl. Data Eng. **29**, 963–976 (2017)

13. Kossmann, D., Ramsak, F., Rost, S.: Shooting stars in the sky: an online algorithm for skyline queries. In: Proceedings of the 28th International Conference on Very Large Data Bases, pp. 275–286. VLDB Endowment (2002)

14. Lee, J., Hwang, S.-W.:. Bskytree: scalable skyline computation using a balanced pivot selection. In: Proceedings of the 13th International Conference on Extending Database Technology, pp. 195–206. ACM (2010)

15. Lee, J., Hwang, S.-W.: Scalable skyline computation using a balanced pivot selection technique. Inf. Syst. **39**, 1–21 (2014)

16. Papadias, D., Tao, Y., Fu, G., Seeger, B.: An optimal and progressive algorithm for skyline queries. In: Proceedings of the 2003 ACM SIGMOD International Conference on Management of Data, pp. 467–478. ACM (2003)

17. Sacharidis, D., Papadopoulos, S., Papadias, D.: Topologically sorted skylines for partially ordered domains. In: IEEE 25th International Conference on Data Engineering, ICDE'09, pp. 1072–1083. IEEE (2009)

18. Trotter, W.T.: Combinatorics and Partially Ordered Sets: Dimension Theory, vol. 6. JHU Press, Baltimore (1992)

19. Wong, R.C.-W., Pei, J., Fu, A.W.-C., Wang, K.: Online skyline analysis with dynamic preferences on nominal attributes. IEEE Trans. Knowl. Data Eng. **21**(1), 35–49 (2009)

20. Zhang, S., Mamoulis, N., Cheung, D.W., Kao, B.: Efficient skyline evaluation over partially ordered domains. Proc. VLDB Endowm. **3**(1–2), 1255–1266 (2010)

Ensuring License Compliance in Linked Data with Query Relaxation

Benjamin Moreau[1] and Patricia Serrano-Alvarado[2(✉)]

[1] OpenDataSoft, Paris, France
Benjamin.Moreau@opendatasoft.com
[2] Nantes University, LS2N, CNRS, UMR6004, 44000 Nantes, France
Patricia.Serrano-Alvarado@univ-nantes.fr

Abstract. When two or more licensed datasets participate in evaluating a federated query, to be reusable, the query result must be protected by a license compliant with each license of the involved datasets. Due to incompatibilities or contradictions among licenses, such a license does not always exist, leading to a query result that cannot be licensed nor reused on a legal basis. We propose to deal with this issue during the federated query processing by dynamically discarding datasets of conflicting licenses. However, this solution may generate an empty query result. To face this problem, we use query relaxation techniques. Our problem statement is, *given a SPARQL query and a federation of licensed datasets, how to guarantee a relevant and non-empty query result whose license is compliant with each license of involved datasets?* To detect and prevent license conflicts, we propose FLiQue, a license-aware query processing strategy for federated query engines. Our challenge is to limit communication costs when the query relaxation process is necessary. Experiments show that FLiQue guarantees license compliance, and if necessary, can find relevant relaxed federated queries with a limited overhead in terms of execution time.

Keywords: Linked data · Federated queries · Licenses · Query relaxation · Compatibility of licenses

1 Introduction and Motivation

The Linked Data is a network of distributed and interlinked data sources. Federated query processing allows to query such a network of live and up-to-date datasets. A *federated SPARQL query* can retrieve information from several RDF data sources distributed across the Linked Data. Since the beginning of Linked Data, licensing has been an important issue [1,36]. To legally facilitate reuse, data owners should systematically associate licenses with resources before sharing or publishing them. There are still several issues to legally access and reuse linked data, as shown in recent Dagstuhl seminars [2,12] and surveys [14].

When two or more licensed datasets participate in evaluating of a federated query, the query result must be protected by a license that is compliant with each

© Springer-Verlag GmbH Germany, part of Springer Nature 2021
A. Hameurlain et al. (Eds.): TLDKS XLIX, LNCS 12920, pp. 97–129, 2021.
https://doi.org/10.1007/978-3-662-64148-4_4

license of involved datasets. Licenses specify precisely the conditions of reuse of data, i.e., what actions are permitted, obliged, and prohibited. Machine-readable licenses are necessary to ensure automatic license compliance. The W3C Open Digital Rights Language (ODRL) [17] allows defining machine-readable licenses. The Data Licenses Clearance Center (DALICC) [25], proposes a library of well-known standard machine-readable licenses.

We consider that a license l_j is compliant with a license l_i if a resource licensed under l_i can be licensed under l_j without violating l_i. If l_j is compliant with l_i, then l_i is compatible with l_j. Unfortunately, it is not always possible to find a license compliant with each license of datasets involved in a federated query [22]. If such a license does not exist, the query result cannot be licensed and, thus, should not be reused nor published.

We consider that a query whose result set cannot be licensed should not be executed. Notice that having the rights to query several datasets individually does not mean having the rights to execute a federated query involving these datasets.

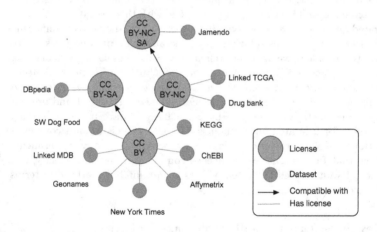

Fig. 1. The compatibility graph of licenses for datasets of LargeRDFBench.

Consider datasets of LargeRDFBench [32], a benchmark for federated query processing. Figure 1 shows the compatibility graph of licenses[1] that protect LargeRDFBench datasets. By transitivity, license CC BY is compatible with itself, with CC BY-SA, CC BY-NC, and CC BY-NC-SA. Thus, datasets protected by CC BY can be queried along with other datasets protected by these licenses. However, the whole set of datasets of Fig. 1 cannot be queried together because there is no license compliant with the fourth licenses. For instance, there is no license with which CC BY-SA and CC BY-NC-SA are both compatible.

---

[1] This compatibility graph conforms to the license compatibility chart shown in https://wiki.creativecommons.org/wiki/Wiki/cc_license_compatibility.

One solution to the incompatibility of licenses is negotiating with data providers to change a conflicting license, e.g., to ask DBpedia to change its license to CC BY or CC BY-NC. Nevertheless, negotiation takes time and is not always possible. A second solution is to discard datasets that are protected by conflicting licenses. However, this solution can lead to a query with an empty result set. To face this problem, we use query relaxation techniques. That is, we use *relaxation rules* to relax the query constraints to match triples of other datasets.

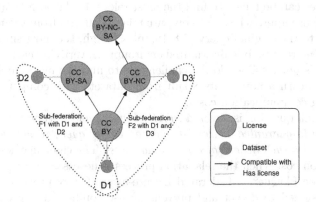

Fig. 2. Compatibility graph of licenses for datasets D1, D2, and D3. As there is no license compatible with licenses of these datasets, sub-federations F1 and F2 should be created. Queries (or relaxed queries) can be evaluated over these sub-federations to produce licensable results.

```
SELECT ?student   WHERE {
    ?student   rdf:type   ex:Student .                      #tp1@{D3}  CC BY–NC
    ?student   ex:enrolledIn   ?course .                    #tp2@{D3}  CC BY–NC
    ?course    ex:heldAt   ex:UniversityOfNantes .  #tp3@{D1}  CC BY
    ex:Ben     ex:teaches   ?course .                      #tp4@{D2}  CC BY–SA
}
```

Listing 1.1. A SPARQL query Q.

Consider the compatibility graph of licenses for datasets D1, D2, and D3 of Fig. 2[2] and the federated query Q of Listing 1.1, which asks for students enrolled in a course held at the University of Nantes taught by *ex:Ben*. The query is annotated with the datasets over which each triple pattern can be evaluated. $D2$ and $D3$ should not be queried together because their licenses are respectively CC BY-SA and CC BY-NC, and there is no license compliant with both. Thus, the result set of the query cannot be licensed. Creating a sub-federation of sources with compatible licenses without $D2$ makes the result set licensable with CC BY-NC or with another license compliant with CC BY-NC (e.g., CC BY-NC-SA).

---

[2] To simplify, we show the same licenses as in Fig. 1. However, a compatibility graph of licenses can contain many more licenses and not limited to Creative Commons ones.

The problem is that the query gives no result because there is no more dataset to evaluate $tp4$. The case is similar with a sub-federation with compatible licenses discarding $D3$ because there is no more dataset to evaluate $tp1$ and $tp2$.

As none subset of licence compatible sources can produce a non-empty result set for Q, we propose using query relaxation techniques. For instance, in such relaxation, instead of asking for students in $tp1$, the federated query could ask for persons, or instead of asking for courses taught by $ex{:}Ben$ in $tp4$, the federated query could ask for courses taught by anybody. The number of possible relaxed queries can be huge. To find the most relevant relaxed federated queries efficiently, we use approaches that compute relaxed queries from the most to the least *similar* to the original query [7, 8, 15, 16]. Though, the most similar queries may produce no results. In a distributed environment, verifying each relaxed federated query is not feasible. So the challenge is to find the most similar relaxed queries that return a non-empty result from datasets with compatible licenses while limiting communication costs.

Our research question is, *given a SPARQL query and a federation of licensed datasets, how to guarantee a relevant and non-empty query result whose license is compliant with each license of involved datasets?* The challenge is to limit the communication cost when the relaxation process is necessary.

We propose FLiQue[3], a Federated License-aware Query processing strategy. FLiQue is designed to detect and prevent license conflicts and gives informed feedback with licenses able to protect a result set of a federated query. If necessary, it applies distributed query relaxation to propose a set of most similar relaxed federated queries whose result set can be licensed. Our solution combines existing approaches, namely, CaLi [22] to maintain a compatibility graph of licenses dynamically and to detect license conflicts, OMBS [8] to efficiently find relaxed queries and data summaries of CostFed [34] to limit communication overhead during the federated query relaxation. Our contributions are:

- an efficient license-aware federated query processing strategy able to relax federated queries,
- an implementation of a license-aware federated query engine, and
- an experimental evaluation of our solution.

In the next, Sect. 2 overviews related works, Sect. 3 introduces FLiQue, Sect. 4 shows experimental results, and Sect. 5 concludes.

2   Related Work

To our knowledge, there is no federated query engine that ensures license compliance with all licenses involved in query execution.

Many works focus on access control over linked data using policy-based [5, 19, 20, 28], view-based [9], or query-rewriting [24] approaches. In these works, datasets are protected by *access control rules* that prevent non-authorized users

---

[3] In French, FLiQue is a homophone of *flic*, which means *cop*.

from querying data of each dataset. These approaches do not resolve our problem statement because having the right to query datasets individually does not mean that it should be possible to execute a federated query involving these datasets.

2.1   Compatibility Graph of Licenses

To know if a result set can be licensed, we need to know the license(s) with whom all licenses of datasets involved in a federated query are compatible. Automatic license compatibility requires machine-readable licenses. License expression languages such as CC REL[4], ODRL, or L4LOD[5] enable fine-grained RDF description of licenses. Works like [31] and [3] use natural language processing to automatically generate RDF licenses from licenses described in natural language. Other works such as [13,30] propose a set of well-known licenses in RDF described in CC REL and ODRL[6]. Thereby, we suppose that there exist consistent licenses described in RDF.

A compatibility graph of licenses contains a set of licenses partially ordered by compatibility. It can be defined by hand using, for instance, the license compatibility chart of Creative Commons. But licenses used in the Linked Data are not limited to Creative Commons licenses. For instance, the license library of DALICC has at least 60 licenses[7].

Works like [37] address the problem of license compatibility and license combination. If licenses are compatible, a new license compliant with combined ones is generated. This approach allows defining the compatibility graph of licenses progressively. However, it does not allow us to know all the compliant licenses that can be used to protect a query result set. That is, all licenses that are compliant to all licenses involved in a query.

In the context of Free Open Source Software (FOSS), [18,38] propose compatibility graphs of well-known licenses. Based on a directed acyclic graph, they propose to detect license violations in existing software packages. They consider that license l_i is compatible with l_j if the graph contains a path from l_i to l_j. The combined software can be protected by the license l_j, possibly with additions from l_i. However, as such a graph is built from a manual interpretation of each license, its generalisation and automation is not possible. In particular, with these approaches it is not possible to add automatically a new license to the compatibility graph of licenses.

CaLi [21,22], is a lattice-based model for license orderings. It automatically positions a license over a set of licenses in terms of compatibility and compliance. The originality of CaLi is to pass through a restrictiveness relation to partially order[8] licenses in terms of compatibility and compliance. In a license, actions

---

[4] https://creativecommons.org/ns.

[5] https://ns.inria.fr/l4lod/.

[6] Creative Commons also proposes its licences in RDF https://github.com/creativecommons/cc.licenserdf/tree/master/cc/licenserdf/licenses.

[7] https://www.dalicc.net/license-library.

[8] A partial order is any binary relation that is reflexive, antisymmetric, and transitive.

(e.g., *read, modify, distribute,* etc.) can be distributed in *status* (e.g., *permissions, duties,* and *prohibitions*). To decide if a license l_i is less restrictive than l_j, it is necessary to know if an action in a status is considered less restrictive than the same action in another status. l_i is said to be less restrictive than l_j if for all actions $a \in A$, the status of a in l_i is less restrictive than the status of a in l_j. The restrictiveness relation between licenses can be obtained automatically, according to the status of actions. Thus, based on lattice-ordered sets, CaLi defines a restrictiveness relation among licenses. If two licenses have a restrictiveness relation, then they may have a compatibility relation too.

To identify the compatibility among licenses, CaLi refines the restrictiveness relation with two types of constraints (license constraints and compatibility constraints). The goal is to take into account the semantics of actions.

- *License constraints* allow to identify non-valid licenses and can be defined as a set of conditions. A condition of a license constraint defines if an action should exist or not in a status. For instance the condition (*cc:CommercialUse* $\notin$ *Duty*) means that a valid license should not have the action *cc:CommercialUse* as a duty. The condition (*cc:ShareAlike* $\notin$ *Prohibition*) means that a valid license should not prohibit the *cc:ShareAlike* action.
- A *compatibility constraint* concerns two licenses where one is more restrictive than another. For instance, consider the action *cc:ShareAlike* which requires that the distribution of derivative works be under the same license only. The compatibility constraint (*cc:ShareAlike* $\notin$ *Duty*) $\notin l_i$ means that l_i is compatible with l_j if the action *cc:ShareAlike* is not a duty in l_i. In another example, the compatibility constraint (*cc:DerivativeWorks* $\notin$ *Prohibition*) $\notin l_i$ means that l_i is compatible with l_j if l_i does not prohibit the distribution of a derivative resource, regardless of the license.

CaLi is able to define all the licenses that can be expressed with a set of actions over a lattice of status[9]. For instance, the CaLi ordering for the set of 7 actions used by Creative Commons has 972 licenses[10]. CaLi can provide all the licenses that can protect a result set ordered by restrictiveness. It can also identify which licenses are in conflict. Knowing the compatibility of a license allows estimating the reusability of the protected resource. On the other hand, knowing the compliance of a license allows knowing to which extent other licensed resources can be reused[11].

In this work, we use CaLi to verify license compliance thanks to its facilities to add dynamically new licenses to the compatibility graph of licenses.

---

[9] A demonstration tool to define, step by step, a compatibility graph of licenses with the CaLi approach can be found here https://saas.ls2n.fr/cali/.

[10] That is $|S|^{|A|}$ minus the licenses discarded by constraints, where S is a set of status and A a set of actions. The three status considered by Creative Commons licenses are: *permissions, duties,* and *prohibitions.*

[11] Next compatibility graphs of licenses illustrate the CaLi approach:
http://cali.priloo.univ-nantes.fr/ld/graph,
http://cali.priloo.univ-nantes.fr/rep/graph.

When the result set of a federated query cannot be licensed, we propose to define sub-federations that avoid license conflicts. If there is no sub-federation able to produce a licensable and non-empty result set for the user query, we propose alternative queries through query relaxation.

2.2 Query Relaxation

Our goal is to provide users with a means to automatically identify new queries that are similar to the user query and whose result set can be licensed.

The OPTIONAL clause of SPARQL[12] was defined to allow query users to add supplementary information to a query solution. That is, if available, the solution of optional triple patterns is added to the query solution. This clause allows users to relax some query's conditions because triple patterns defined as optional extend the query result of the non-optional triple patterns. As this clause is not added dynamically (query users define which triple patterns are OPTIONAL), it cannot be useful when a license compatibility problem arises during the source selection phase of the query execution.

Query relaxation techniques are used to provide an alternative for queries producing no result. Transformations are applied to user queries to relax constraints in order to generalize the query so that it can produce more answers. The solution espace grows in a combinatorial way with the number of relaxation steps and the size of the query. Existing works propose techniques to reduce this espace producing the most *similar* relaxed queries. We are interested in query relaxation techniques that could be used to relax efficiently a federated query.

There are works that focus on symbolic forms of semantic similarity that can be represented with graph patterns [7]. They identify similar entities based on common graph patterns. Their approach is a symbolic form of the k-nearest neighbours where numerical distances are replaced by graph patterns that provide an intelligible representation of how similar two nodes are. The drawback of this approach is that it needs all possible answers of relaxed queries (*i.e.*, the entities). As we do not consider a centralized RDF graph with all datasources, this solution applied to a distributed environnement would be very expensive in communication and execution time.

Other works focus on ontology-based similarity measures to retrieve additional answers of possible relevance [8,15,16]. They use logical relaxation of the query conditions based on RDFS entailment and RDFS ontologies.

[16] proposes a RELAX clause as a generalization of the OPTIONAL clause for the conjunctive part of a SPARQL query. Their goal is to relax the query without simply dropping the optional triple pattern. The idea consists of relaxation rules that use information from the ontology; these include relaxing a class to its super-class, relaxing a property to its super-property, etc. Other relaxations can be entailed without an ontology, which include replacing constants with variables, suppressing join dependencies and dropping triple patterns. All possible relaxed queries are organized in a lattice called *relaxation graph*. They

---

[12] https://www.w3.org/TR/rdf-sparql-query/#OptionalMatching.

propose to rank the results of a query based on how closely they satisfy the query. Their ranking is based on the relaxation graph, in which relaxed versions of the original query are ordered from less to more general from a logical standpoint. Given two relaxed queries of the user query, if one is subsumed by the other, then the former relaxed query is better. Subsumption is based on the hypothesis that if c_1 is a subclass of c_2, c_2 is the class that subsumes c_1 and c_2 (idem for subproperties). The size of the relaxation graph grows combinatorially with the number of relaxation rules, the richness of the ontology, and the relaxation possibilities of each triple pattern in the original query.

[8,15] focus on obtaining a certain number of alternative results (top-k) by relaxing a query that produces no results. Their challenge is to execute as less as possible relaxed queries to obtain the top-k results. Relaxed queries are executed in a similarity-based rank order to avoid executing all relaxed queries in the relaxation graph. *Information content* [29] is used to measure the *similarity* between a relaxed query and the original query. That is, statistical information about the concerned dataset, like the number of entities per class and the number of triples per property. Nevertheless, the number of failing relaxed queries executed before obtaining the top-k results can be large. Thus, it is necessary to identify unnecessary relaxations that do not generate new answers. Relaxed queries containing unnecessary relaxation should not be executed.

[15] proposes OBFS (Optimized Best First Search algorithm) to identify unnecessary relaxations in a similarity-based relaxation graph. It is based on the *selectivity* of relaxations using the number of entities per class or the number of triples per property. If the selectivity is the same before and after the relaxation, the relaxation is considered unnecessary. That is, if the number of entities of a class is equal to the number of entities of its super-class, then the class relaxation does not generate new answers. The same idea is used for property relaxation.

[8] proposes OMBS (Optimized Minimal-failing-sub-queries-Based Search algorithm) as an improvement to OBFS. The contribution of OMBS is to identify the minimal sets of triple patterns in failing queries that fail to return answers. These failing sets of triple patterns are called Minimal Failing Sub-queries (MFS). MFS existing in a query must be relaxed, otherwise, the query fails in producing results. Relaxed queries where the MFS are not relaxed are considered unnecessary. OMBS defines optimal similarity-based relaxation graphs where relaxed queries producing no results (based on MFS), or not new results (based on selectivity) are not executed.

Table 1 overviews these three approaches from four dimensions: (1) RDFS properties used, (2) similarity definition, (3) information needed for the query relaxation process and (4) methods used to prune the relaxation graph.

1. The **RDFS properties** used in the relaxation rules proposed by [16], concern the domain, the range, the subproperties and the subclasses of a class used in a triple pattern. [15] and [8], base their relaxation rules only on the subproperties and subclasses of a class used in a triple pattern.
2. The **similarity definition** of [16], is only based on the relations of the relaxation graph, where relaxed queries are ordered based on the subsumption

Table 1. An analysis of existing approaches about ontology-based query relaxation.

	RDFS properties	Similarity definition	Information needed	Pruning method
[16]	rdfs:domain rdfs:range rdfs:subPropertyOf rdfs:subClassOf	Subsumption relation among relaxed queries	Ontology	Discards indirect ontology relations
[15]	rdfs:subPropertyOf rdfs:subClassOf	Based on information content measures between the original query and the relaxed queries	Ontology and dataset statistics	Based on the number of instances Based on join dependency
[8]	rdfs:subPropertyOf rdfs:subClassOf	Based on information content measures between the original query and the relaxed queries	Ontology and dataset statistics	Based on failure causes of triple patterns

relation of their result sets. This partial order makes that it is not always possible to compare two relaxed queries. [15] and [8] use information content measures to obtain a total order between the original query and the relaxed queries. Such similarity is computed using statistical information of the concerned dataset, e.g., the number of entities per class and the number of triples per property.

3. Concerning the **information needed**, these works use the dataset ontology. [15] and [8] also use dataset statistics to calculate the information content of relaxed queries.

4. For **pruning the relaxation graph**, [16] avoids redundant query relaxation by reducing ontologies, e.g., it uses the ontology without saturation. [15] uses the number of entities per classes and the number of triples per properties to identify query relaxation that does not generate new results. Finally, [8] identifies the set of triple patterns that fail to return results. Thus, it only keeps relaxed queries that do not contain failing triple patterns.

We consider that these three approaches [8,15,16] can be used to relax federated queries because they can produce relaxed queries using the dataset ontology and statistical information (to calculate selectivity) without needing the RDF graph (i.e., the instances). We use OMBS to find relaxed queries because it optimizes obtaining the number of relaxed queries that potentially give non-empty results.

2.3 Data Summaries

In this work, we need *data summaries* to calculate similarity measures (based on information content), selectivity, but also to limit the communication overhead, during the *distributed query relaxation* process. A very complete survey of the state-of-the about summarization methods for semantic RDF graphs is proposed in [4]. In federated query processing, some federated query engines, use statistics to reduce the number of requests sent to data sources during the source selection and the query optimization steps [10,27,33,34]. Analysis of state-of-the-art federated query engines can be found in [23,26,32].

VoID[13], is the Vocabulary of Interlinked Datasets [6]. It allows to formally describe linked RDF datasets with metadata like contact, topic, licenses, SPARQL endpoint, url of data dumps, basic statistics, etc. In particular, with VoID descriptions is possible to describe dataset instances, i.e., the number of instances of a given class and the number of triples that have a certain predicate.

DARQ [27] (from Distributed ARQ)[14] is the first query engine that allows querying multiple, distributed SPARQL endpoints. DARQ introduced service descriptions which provide a declarative description of the data available from an SPARQL endpoint[15]. Service descriptions include statistical information used for query optimization represented in RDF. A service description describes the data available from a data source in form of *capabilities*. Capabilities define what kind of triple patterns can be answered by the data source. The definition of capabilities is based on predicates. Statistical information includes the total number of triples in data sources and average selectivity estimates for combinations of subject, predicate, and object.

SPLENDID [10], a query optimization strategy for federating SPARQL endpoints, uses VoID descriptions of datasets to speed-up query processing. The statistical information for every predicate and type are organized in inverted indexes which map predicates and types to a set of tuples containing the data source and the number of occurrences in the data source. For triple patterns with bound variables which are not covered in the VoID statistics, SPLENDID uses SPARQL ASK queries including the triple pattern to all pre-selected data sources and remove failing sources. This improves the source selection efficiency.

HIBISCuS [33], a join-aware source selection algorithm, discards dataset that are relevant for a triple pattern, but that do not contribute to a query result. It proposes detailed data summaries, *dataset capabilities*, containing all the distinct properties with all the URI authorities of their subjects and objects. HIBISCuS has been implemented over the federated query engines FedX [35] and SPLENDID.

CostFed [34], an index-assisted federated engine for SPARQL endpoints, extends and improves the join-aware source selection of HIBISCuS by considering URI prefixes instead of URI authorities. It uses such prefixes to prune irrelevant data sources more effectively than the state-of-the-art approaches. In particular, HIBISCuS fails to prune the data sources that share the same URI authority. CostFed overcomes this problem by using source specific sets of strings that many URIs in the data source begin with (these strings are the prefixes of the URI strings). The CostFed query planner also considers the skew distribution of subjects and objects per predicate in each data source. In addition, separate cardinality estimation is used for multi-valued predicates. The dataset capabilities calculated by CostFed are more efficient than other state-of-the-art approaches, its source selection chooses, in general, more pertinently the data sources for each query.

---

[13] https://www.w3.org/TR/void/.

[14] DARQ is an extension of ARQ http://jena.sourceforge.net/ARQ/.

[15] The VoID vocabulary was proposed after DARQ.

In our work we use VoID descriptions to calculate similarity measures and the join-aware source selection of CostFed to limit communication costs during the distributed query relaxation process.

3   A Federated License-Aware Query Processing Strategy

To legally facilitate reuse of query results when retrieving information from several RDF data sources distributed across the Linked Data, we propose FLiQue, a federated license-aware query processing strategy to detect and prevent license conflicts. The goal of FLiQue is to empower federated query engines to produce licensable query results.

A federation is a set of SPARQL endpoints. We consider that a sub-federation is a subset of endpoints of a federation.

FLiQue gives informed feedback with the set of licenses that can protect a result set of a federated query. When the result set of a federated query cannot be licensed, FLiQue defines sub-federations that avoid license conflicts. If there is no sub-federation able to produce a licensable and non-empty result set, FLiQue proposes alternative relaxed federated queries.

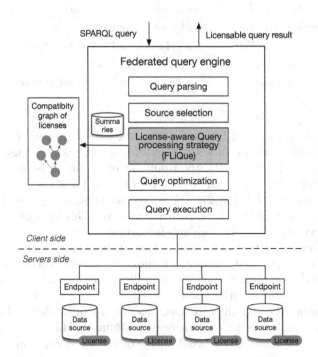

Fig. 3. Global architecture of a federated license-aware query engine using FLiQue.

Figure 3 shows the global architecture of a license-aware federated query engine using FLiQue. We consider that there exist a federation of endpoints whose datasetes are associated to licenses[16]. FLiQue is located between the source selection and the query optimization functions of a federated query engine. A join-aware source selection [34], selects the *capable datasets* for each triple pattern of a query. Using a compatibility graph of licenses [22], we search for licenses compliant with each license of the chosen capable datasets. Then, the query is executed and the result set returned with the licenses that can protect it. If no compliant license exists, we identify the license conflicts and define sub-federations that avoid these conflicts. If one sub-federation can produce a licensable and non-empty result, the query is executed. Otherwise, based on the OMBS approach [8], we propose to the query issuer a set of relaxed queries whose result sets are licensable and non-empty.

Several sub-federations may produce a licensable and non-empty result. In that case, it is possible to choose the sub-federation that produces a result set licensable by the least restrictive license[17].

Table 2. Dataset D1 containing courses. D1 has licence CC BY.

Subject	Predicate	Object
ex:UniversityOfNantes	rdf:type	ex:University
ex:SemanticWeb	rdf:type	ex:Course
ex:SemanticWeb	ex:heldAt	ex:UniversityOfNantes
ex:Databases	rdf:type	ex:Course
ex:Databases	ex:heldAt	ex:UniversityOfNantes

Consider the query Q of Listing 1.1, and the federation containing datasets $D1$, $D2$, and $D3$ shown in Tables 2, 3 and 4. As there is no license compliant with the licenses of $D2$ and $D3$, the result set of Q cannot be licensed. Thus, our strategy defines the sub-federations $F1 = \{D1, D2\}$ and $F2 = \{D1, D3\}$ that avoid license conflicts (cf. Fig. 2). The source selection for Q over $F1$ and $F2$ fails to obtain a data source for each triple pattern. This launches a process of federated query relaxation for each sub-federation.

To avoid verifying that the result set of an important number of relaxed queries is not empty, our strategy defines, by sub-federation, an optimal similarity-based relaxation graph. When we find one licensable and non-empty relaxed query, we stop the relaxation process.

Figure 4 shows Q and three relaxed queries. Figure 5 shows the ontology used in our example. As we explain next, $Q'4b$ and $Q'4d$ are the most similar licensable, and non-empty relaxed query for the sub-federations $F1$ and $F2$

---

[16] Datasets without licenses can be associated with the most permissive license (e.g., CC Zero, and ODbL) or can be discarded from the federation.

[17] Other choices could be defined, for example, based on the cardinality estimations of result sets or based on the number of involved data sources.

Table 3. Dataset D2 containing teachers and students. D2 has licence CC BY-SA.

Subject	Predicate	Object
ex:Ben	rdf:type	ex:Teacher
ex:Ben	rdf:type	ex:Person
ex:Ben	ex:attends	ex:SemanticWeb
ex:Ben	ex:teaches	ex:SemanticWeb
ex:Mary	rdf:type	ex:Teacher
ex:Mary	rdf:type	ex:Person
ex:Mary	ex:attends	ex:Databases
ex:Mary	ex:teaches	ex:Databases
my:William	rdf:type	ex:Student
my:William	rdf:type	ex:Person
my:William	ex:attends	ex:Databases
my:William	ex:enrolledIn	ex:Databases

Table 4. Dataset D3 containing students. D3 has licence CC BY-NC.

Subject	Predicate	Object
ex:Elsa	rdf:type	ex:Student
ex:Elsa	rdf:type	ex:Person
ex:Elsa	ex:attends	ex:SemanticWeb
ex:Elsa	ex:enrolledIn	ex:SemanticWeb

respectively. Identifying sub-federations with compatible licenses and queries (or relaxed queries) that produce non-empty results are the contributions of FLiQue.

In the next, Sect. 3.1 shows the relaxation techniques we use. Section 3.2 presents the information content measures that allow us to rank relaxed queries. Section 3.3 shows the data summaries that allow limiting communication costs. Finally, Sect. 3.4 explains the global algorithm of FLiQue and how we define the similarity-based relaxation graph.

Q (original query) — **Result no licensable**

```
SELECT * WHERE {
  ?student   rdf:type ex:Student .                    #tp1@{D3}
  ?student   ex:enrolledIn ?course .                   #tp2@{D3}
  ?course    ex:heldAt ex:UniversityOfNantes .         #tp3@{D1}
  ex:Ben     ex:teaches ?course .                      #tp4@{D2}
}
```

Q'3b4b with Simple relaxations — Sim=0.44 in F1 — **Result licensable if D3 excluded**

```
SELECT * WHERE {
  ?student   rdf:type ex:Student .                    #tp1@{D2,D3}
  ?student   ex:enrolledIn ?course .                   #tp2@{D2,D3}
  ?course    ex:heldAt ?y .                            #tp3b@{D1}
  ?x         ex:teaches ?course .                      #tp4'b@{D2}
}
```

Q'4b with Simple relaxation — Sim=0.66 in F1 — **Result licensable if D3 excluded**

```
SELECT * WHERE {
  ?student   rdf:type ex:Student .                        #tp1@{D2,D3}
  ?student   ex:enrolledIn ?course .                       #tp2@{D2,D3}
  ?course    ex:heldAt ex:UniversityOfNantes .             #tp3@{D1}
  ?x         ex:teaches ?course .                          #tp4'b@{D2}
}
```

Q'4d with Simple and Property relaxations — Sim=0,33 in F2 — **Result licensable if D2 excluded**

```
SELECT * WHERE {
  ?student   rdf:type ex:Student .                        #tp1@{D2,D3}
  ?student   ex:enrolledIn ?course .                       #tp2@{D2,D3}
  ?course    ex:heldAt ex:UniversityOfNantes .             #tp3@{D1}
  ?x         ex:attends ?course .                          #tp4'd@{D2,D3}
}
```

Fig. 4. Example of SPARQL query Q and some relaxed queries Q'.

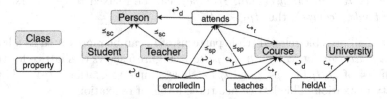

Fig. 5. Ontology representing courses in a university. $\preceq_{sc}$ is rdfs:subClassOf, $\preceq_{sp}$ is rdfs:subPropertyOf, $\hookleftarrow_d$ is rdfs:domain, and $\hookrightarrow_r$ is rdfs:range.

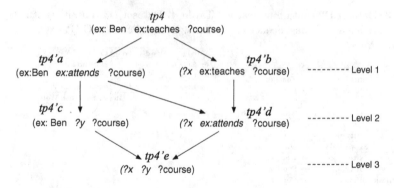

Fig. 6. Relaxation lattice of triple pattern $tp4$ of query Q.

3.1 Query Relaxation Techniques Used in FLiQue

In this work, we use query relaxation using RDFS entailment and RDFS ontologies. We consider that ontologies of datasets are accessible and that SPARQL endpoints expose saturated RDF data (or support on-the-fly entailment) according to the RDFS entailment rules rdfs7 and rdfs9. We use the relaxations of triple patterns and queries as proposed in [15].

Triple Pattern Relaxation. Given two triple patterns tp and tp', tp' is a relaxed triple pattern obtained from tp, denoted $tp \prec tp'$, by applying one or more triple pattern relaxations. We use the three following triple pattern relaxations:

- *Simple relaxation* replaces a constant of a triple pattern by a variable.
  For example, $tp_4 = \langle ex{:}Ben, ex{:}teaches, \text{?}course \rangle$, can be relaxed to $tp'_4 = \langle \text{?}x, ex{:}teaches, \text{?}course \rangle$, thus $tp_4 \prec_s tp'_4$.
- *Type relaxation* replaces a class C of a triple pattern with its super-class C'. It is based on the rdfs9 rule (rdfs:subClassOf).
  For example, $tp_1 = \langle \text{?}student, rdf{:}type, ex{:}Student \rangle$, can be relaxed to $tp'_1 = \langle \text{?}student, rdf{:}type, ex{:}Person \rangle$, thus $tp_1 \prec_{sc} tp'_1$.
- *Property relaxation* replaces a property P of a triple pattern with its super-property P'. It is based on the rdfs7 rule (rdfs:subPropertyOf). For example, $tp_1 = \langle \text{?}student, ex{:}enrolledIn, \text{?}course \rangle$, can be relaxed to $tp'_1 = \langle \text{?}student, ex{:}attends, \text{?}course \rangle$, thus $tp_1 \prec_{sp} tp'_1$.

The set of all possible relaxed triple patterns of tp can be represented as a lattice called a *relaxation lattice of a triple pattern*. Figure 6 shows this lattice for triple pattern $tp4$ of Q. $tp4'b$, $tp4'c$ and $tp4'e$ show simple relaxations. $tp4'a$ shows a property relaxation. This lattice has three levels of relaxation.

Query Relaxation. Given two queries Q and Q', Q' is a relaxed query obtained from Q, denoted $Q \prec Q'$, by applying one or more triple pattern relaxations to triple patterns of Q. $\prec$ is a partial order over the set of all possible relaxed queries of Q. This order can be represented as a lattice, called a *relaxation lattice of a query* (or relaxation graph). Figure 4 shows the query Q and three relaxed queries of its relaxation graph where, $Q \prec Q'4b \prec Q'4d$ and $Q \prec Q'4b \prec Q'3b4b$.

3.2   Information Content Measures Used in FLiQue

Analyzing all relaxed queries is time-consuming and unnecessary. We use *information content measures* to compute the similarity of relaxed queries to the original query. To avoid the analysis of an important number relaxed queries, our approach generates and executes relaxed queries from the most to the least similar. This execution allows to verify that the result set is not empty. It is stopped when the first result is returned. We use the *similarity mesures* proposed in [15], and explained in the following.

Similarity Between Terms. FLiQue uses three similarity measures for terms in a triple pattern. They correspond to the three relaxations described in Sect. 3.1.

- *Similarity between classes* is $Sim(C, C') = \frac{IC(C')}{IC(C)}$ where $IC(C)$ is the information content of C: $-logPr(C)$, where $Pr(C) = \frac{|Instances(C)|}{|Instances|}$ is the probability of finding an instance of class C in the RDF dataset.
  For example, if the subject or object of a triple pattern is a class c_1 and is relaxed to its super class c_2 using type relaxation, the similarity between c_1 and c_2 is $Sim(c_1, c_2)$.
  Notice that, the similarity between classes is zero when all the instances in the RDF dataset belong to the super class C', i.e., $Pr(C') = 1$ and thus $-logPr(C') = 0$. Notice also that the similarity between classes is undefined when all the instances belong to the super class C', and none to C, i.e., $Pr(C) = 0$ and thus $-logPr(C') = undefined$.
- *Similarity between properties* is $Sim(P, P') = \frac{IC(P')}{IC(P)}$ where $IC(P)$ is the information content of P: $-logPr(P)$, where $Pr(P) = \frac{|Triples(P)|}{|Triples|}$ is the probability of finding a property of P in triples of the RDF dataset.
  For example, if the predicate of a triple pattern is a property p_1 and is relaxed to its super property p_2 using property relaxation, the similarity between p_1 and p_2 is $Sim(p_1, p_2)$.
  Notice that as the similarity between classes, the similarity between properties is zero when all the triples in the RDF dataset belong to the super property P', and the similarity between properties is undefined when all the triples belong to the super property P', and none to P.
- *Similarity between constants and variables* is $Sim(T_{const}, T_{var}) = 0$.
  For example, if the object of a triple pattern t_{const} is a class and is relaxed to a variable t_{var} using simple relaxation, the similarity between t_{const} and t_{var} is 0.

Similarity Between Triple Patterns. Given two triple patterns tp and tp', such that $tp \prec tp'$, the similarity of the triple pattern tp' to the original triple pattern tp, denoted $Sim(tp, tp')$, is the average of the similarities between the terms of the triple patterns:

$$Sim(tp, tp') = \frac{1}{3}.Sim(s, s') + \frac{1}{3}.Sim(p, p') + \frac{1}{3}.Sim(o, o')$$

where s, p, o, s', p' and o' are respectively the subject, predicate and object of the triple pattern tp and the relaxed triple pattern tp'. If tp' and tp'' are two relaxations obtained from tp and $tp' \prec tp''$ then $Sim(tp, tp') \geq Sim(tp, tp'')$.

Similarity Between Queries. Given two queries Q and Q', such that $Q \prec Q'$, the similarity of the original query Q' to the original query Q, denoted $Sim(Q, Q')$, is the product of the similarity between triple patterns of the query:

$$Sim(Q, Q') = \prod_{i=1}^{n} w_i.Sim(tp_i, tp'_i)$$

Where tp_i is a triple pattern of Q, tp'_i a triple pattern of Q', $tp_i \prec tp'_i$, and $w_i \in [0, 1]$ is the weight of triple patterns tp_i. Weight can be specified by the user to take into account the importance of a triple pattern tp_i in query Q. Thus $Sim(Q, Q') \in [0, 1]$ is a function that defines a total order among relaxed queries.

This similarity function is monotone, i.e., given two relaxed queries $Q'(tp'_1, ..., tp'_n)$ and $Q''(tp''_1, ..., tp''_n)$ of the user query Q, if $Q' \prec Q''$ then $Sim(Q, Q') \geq Sim(Q, Q'')$.

Considering the query Q and datasets D1 and D2, $Sim(Q, Q'4b) = 0.66$ is greater than $Sim(Q, Q'3b4b) = 0.44$. This verifies the ordering of these relaxed queries, $Q'4b \prec Q'3b4b$, where $Q'4b$ is analyzed first to see if it returns some results.

3.3   Data Summaries Used in FLiQue

FLiQue collects dataset summaries and ontologies before executing queries. A data summary is a compact structure that represents an RDF dataset. Using dataset statistics and dataset capabilities as in [34], allow us to limit communication cost in the similarity calculation and the source selection process.

Dataset statistics contain VoID descriptions, such as the number of entities per class and the number of triples per property. Having dataset statistics is twofold; they allow computing similarities, and they help in the source selection process. Tables 5 and 6 show respectively statistics about properties and classes for sub-federations F1 and F2. In Table 5, the property *ex:teaches* has no triples in F2. So there is no data source for *tp4* and *tp4'b* (cf. Fig. 6). That allows to identify whatever query including these triple patterns as failing queries if executed over F2.

Dataset capabilities contain the properties of a dataset with the common prefixes of their subjects and objects. We recall that prefixes are strings that many URIs in the data source begin with. The *rdf:type* property, is treated differently. The prefixes of its objects are replaced by all the classes used in the dataset. Dataset capabilities are used in the source selection process. The goal is to discard datasets that individually return results for a triple pattern, but that fail to perform joins with other triple patterns of the query. For multiple triple patterns of a query sharing a variable, the dataset capabilities allow identifying data sources that do not share the same URIs prefixes and thus whose joins yield empty results. This information allows performing an optimal source selection by limiting the communication with the data sources. Table 7 shows the capabilities of F1 and F2.

Consider *tp4'a*: ⟨*ex:Ben ex:attends ?cours*⟩
   Statistics in Table 5 show one triple for *ex:attends* in F2 but capabilities of this property in F2 show only one subject prefix that is *ex: Elsa*, not *ex:Ben*. Thus, capabilities of F2 allow to identify *tp4'a* as failing if executed over F2.

Consider also the join *tp3 . tp4'c*, that is a subject-object join:
   {?course ex:heldAt ex:UniversityOfNantes . ex:Ben ?y ?course }
   Statistics in Table 5 show two triples for *ex:heldAt* in both sub-federations. But, analyzing the subject and object capabilities of whatever property (the predicate of *tp4'c* is a variable) of F2, we notice that when there exists *ex:SemanticWeb* in the object, the subject contains *ex: Elsa*, not *ex:Ben*, so the join dependency on *?course* cannot be satisfied. Thus, thanks to the dataset capabilities of F2, we identify that whatever query with this join will be identified as failing query. Notice that this join over F1 cannot be discarded with the statistiques and dataset capabilities. Indeed, this join returns results over F1.

3.4   Global **FLiQue** algorithm and the Similarity-Based Relaxation Graph

Algorithm 1 shows the global approach of FLiQue. After a process of source selection for a federated query Q, FLiQue checks if the result set can be licensed (Line 5). If that is the case ($\mathcal{L} == \emptyset$ is false), the query plan as long as the set of licences that can protect the result set are returned (Line 18). Then the query is optimized and executed as usual.

When the result set cannot be licensed because there is no license compliant to every license of selected datasets, FLiQue calls for a source selection over each sub-federation (Line 6). Each sub-federation that can evaluate the query is returned as long as with the corresponding set of compliant licenses (Line 10).

If all source selections fail (Line 11), FLiQue relaxes the query conditions and proposes alternative relaxed federated queries. We consider that a source selection process fails if it does not identify at least one data source to evaluate each triple pattern of the federated query. Based on techniques of query relaxation in

Table 5. Statistics of properties in federations F1 and F2.

Property	Number of triples	
	F1 = {D1, D2}	F2 = {D1, D3}
ex:enrolledIn	1	1
ex:teaches	2	0
ex:heldAt	2	2
ex:attends	3	1
rdf:type	9	5
Total	17	9

Table 6. Statistics of classes in federations F1 and F2.

Class	Number of entities	
	F1 = {D1, D2}	F2 = {D1, D3}
ex:University	1	1
ex:Student	1	1
ex:Teacher	2	0
ex:Course	2	2
ex:Person	3	1
Total	6	4

Table 7. Capabilities of sub-federations F1 and F2.

Property	F1 = {D1, D2}		F2 = {D1, D3}	
	subjPrefixes	objPrefixes	subjPrefixes	objPrefixes
rdf:type	ex: my: William	ex:Person ex:Student ex:Teacher	ex:	ex:University ex:Course ex:Student ex:Person
ex:heldAt	ex:	ex:UniversityOfNantes	ex:	ex:UniversityOfNantes
ex:attends	ex: my: William	ex:	ex: Elsa	ex:SemanticWeb
ex:teaches	ex:	ex:		
ex:enrolledIn	my: William	ex:Database	ex: Elsa	ex:SemanticWeb

RDF [8] (Line 13), FLiQue proposes to the query issuer a relaxed query for each sub-federation whose result set is licensable and non-empty (line 16).

The result of the algorithm is a set of triplets representing what we call *candidate queries*. A triplet $\langle Q, E, \mathcal{L} \rangle$ is a query Q that returns a non-empty result set when executed on a sub-federation of endpoints E that can be protected by a set of licenses $\mathcal{L}$.

Algorithm 1: The global approach of FLiQue.

---

1 **Function** *FLiQue(Q, F, E, S, C)*:

    Data: Q: RDF Query,

    F: Federation of endpoints,

    $E \subseteq F$: Set of pertinent endpoints for Q,

    S: Dataset summaries,

    C: Compatibility graph of licenses.

    Result: A set of tuples $\langle Q, E, \mathcal{L} \rangle$ representing candidate queries with corresponding pertinent endpoints and compliant licenses.

2     $Fs = \{F' \subseteq F \mid compliantLicenses(F', C) \neq \emptyset\}$

3     $Candidates = \emptyset$

4     $\mathcal{L} = \text{compliantLicenses}(E,C)$

5   **if** $\mathcal{L} == \emptyset$ **then**

6   **for** $F' \in Fs$ **do**

7             $E' = sourceSelection(Q, F', S)$

8   **if** E' *can evaluate* Q **then**

                // The original query can be executed on E'.

9                 $\mathcal{L} = \text{compliantLicenses}(E',C)$

10                $Candidates = Candidates \cup \langle Q, E', \mathcal{L} \rangle$

11   **if** $Candidates == \emptyset$ **then**

            // Compute most similar queries.

12   **for** $F' \in Fs$ **do**

13                $Q' = \text{queryRelaxation}(Q, F', S)$

14                $E' = sourceSelection(Q', F', S)$

                // The relaxed query Q' can be executed on E'.

15                $\mathcal{L} = \text{compliantLicenses}(E',C)$

16                $Candidates = Candidates \cup \langle Q', E', \mathcal{L} \rangle$

17   **else**

        // The original query can be executed on E.

18         $Candidates = \{\langle Q, E, \mathcal{L} \rangle\}$

19   **return** $Candidates$

When the distributed query relaxation is necessary, we define an optimal similarity-based relaxation graph by sub-federation. The goal is to avoid verifying that the result set of an important number of relaxed queries is not empty. Relaxed queries are generated and executed from the most to the least similar. When we find one licensable and non-empty candidate query, we stop the relaxation process. OMBS [8] guarantees that a candidate query is the most similar to Q for a sub-federation.

In the following, we explain how FLiQue finds the candidate query for the sub-federation F2. First, the algorithm computes the MFS of the original query, $\text{MFS}(Q) = \{\text{ex:Ben ex:teaches ?course}\}$. It contains only $tp4$ because $F2$ does not contain a data source to evaluate $tp4$. Using the MFS, the algorithm considers only relaxed queries that contain a relaxation of $tp4$.

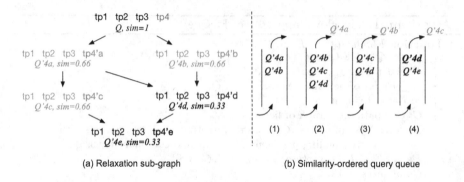

(a) Relaxation sub-graph   (b) Similarity-ordered query queue

Fig. 7. Relaxation sub-graph of Q over $F2$ with relaxations of $tp4$.

The relaxation algorithm uses a query queue ordered by similarity. This query queue gives the analysis order of relaxed queries. Figure 7(a) shows a relaxation sub-graph where $tp4$, that is the MFS, is relaxed, and Fig. 7(b) shows the analysis process of relaxed queries with the query queue (failing relaxed queries are in gray).

Relaxed queries of the first level, $Q'4a$ and $Q'4b$, are generated and inserted in the queue, see (1) in Fig. 7(b). The most similar relaxed query $Q'4a$ is analyzed. It is identified as a failing query (cf. Sect. 3.3), thus it is relaxed, so $Q'4c$, and $Q'4d$ are generated and inserted in the query queue (2). Then, the first relaxed query in the queue, now $Q'4b$, is analyzed. It is also identified as a failing query so it is relaxed in $Q'4d$, which is already in the queue (3). Then, the first relaxed query in the queue, now $Q'4c$, is analyzed and identified as a failing query, so it is relaxed into $Q'4e$, which is inserted in the queue (4). Then, the first relaxed query in the queue, now $Q'4d$, is analyzed. It is not identified as a failing query. It is executed, and it returns a non-empty result set. Thus, $Q'4d$ (in bold) is the candidate query of query Q for the federation $F2$, and the relaxation process stops.

The MFS and the failing relaxed queries of this example are identified thanks to data summaries without making requests to data sources (cf. Sect. 3.3).

In this example, we found a candidate query only with the relaxation of $tp4$. But the relaxation may continue until all triple patterns are composed of variables. A threshold of similarity can be used to avoid such a worst case.

Figure 4 shows the candidate query $Q'4d$, whose similarity with Q is 0.33. This query asks for students attending a course held at the University of Nantes.

The candidate query for federation $F1$ is $Q'4b$, whose similarity with Q is 0.66. Figure 4 shows $Q'4b$, this query asks for students enrolled in a course held at the University of Nantes and taught by someone.

CC BY-SA can protect relaxed queries for $F1$. Relaxed queries for $F2$ can be protected by CC BY-NC but also by CC BY-NC-SA because both licenses are compliant with licenses of $D1$ and $D3$. Table 8 shows the feedback returned to the query issuer so that she can choose which query to execute.

Table 8. FLiQue feedback with candidate queries for the user query Q.

Sub-federation	Query	Similarity	Compliant licenses
F1={D1, D2}	Q'4b	0.66	CC BY-SA
F2={D1, D3}	Q'4d	0.33	CC BY-NC, CC BY-NC-SA

4   Experimental Evaluation

The goal of our experimental evaluation is to measure the overhead produced by the implementation of our proposal. In particular, (a) when the result set of the original query is licensable, and (b) when the original query is relaxed.

4.1   Setup and Implementation

FLiQue is implemented over CostFed, which relies on a join-aware triple-wise source selection. Recent studies show that the source selection of CostFed least overestimates the set of capable data sources, with a small number of ASK requests [32,34]. These performances make CostFed a good choice for our license-aware query processing strategy. The join ordering of CostFed is based on left-deep join trees. It implements bind and symmetric hash joins.

Our test environment uses LargeRDFBench [32]. A benchmark with more than 1 billion triples for SPARQL endpoints. This benchmark contains 32 federated queries that are executed over a federation of 11 interlinked data sources (we consider the three Linked TCGA datasets as only one). We identified the license of each dataset (cf. Fig. 1). We use a Creative Commons CaLi ordering [22] to verify compatibility and compliance among licenses.

LargeRDFBench was defined to evaluate and compare federated query engines. It is composed of 14 simple queries (S1–S14), 10 complex queries (C1–C10), and 8 large queries (L1–L8). The number of triple patterns in queries varies from 2 to 12 (the average is 7). Simple queries range from 2 to 7 triple patterns and their execution time is small (few seconds). Complex queries add constraints to simple queries. They range from 8 to 12 triple patterns and their evaluation is costly in time (few minutes). Large queries were defined to be evaluated over large datasets and involve large intermediate result sets. They range from 5 to 11 triple patterns and their evaluation is very costly (it can exceeds one hour).

In our experiments we are not interested in obtaining the complete query results of all these queries but in showing that preserving licences during federated query processing is possible. Thus, queries were executed until obtaining the first result (LIMIT 1 was added to all queries).

Our experiment runs on a single machine with a 160xIntel(R) Xeon(R) CPU E7-8870 v4 2.10 GHz 1,5 Tb RAM. Each dataset of LargeRDFBench is saturated and made available using a single-threaded Virtuoso endpoint in a docker container with 4 Gb RAM. Between each query execution, caches are reset.

Table 9. The 16 queries of LargeRDFBench whose result set cannot be licensed. DBP (DBpedia), DB (Drug bank), TCGA (Linked TCGA), JA (Jamendo).

Conflicting sources	Conflicting licenses	Queries
DBP, DB	CC BY-SA, CC BY-NC	S1, **S10**, **C9**
DBP, TCGA	CC BY-SA, CC BY-NC	**L7**
DBP, JA	CC BY-SA, CC BY-NC-SA	**L6**
DBP, DB, TCGA	CC BY-SA, CC BY-NC	**C10**
DBP, DB, TCGA, JA	CC BY-SA, CC BY-NC, CC BY-NC-SA	S6, **S8**, S9, C3, **C5**, **C8**, L1, L3, **L5**, **L8**

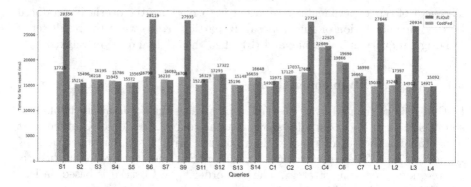

Fig. 8. Average time to get the first result of the 22 queries of LargeRDFBench that can produce a licensable result set without relaxation.

4.2 Performance of FLiQuevs CostFed

To measure the overhead produced by FLiQue, we compare two different federated query engines: CostFed and CostFed+FLiQue (that we call FLiQue to simplify). They correspond to the original implementation of CostFed[18] and our extension of CostFed that includes FLiQue[19]. CostFed executes a query without considering licenses while FLiQue guarantees license compliance of the result set.

We executed all queries 5 times with each federated query engine. We measured the time in milliseconds to return the first result of each query.

Using the capable data sources by query, and the compatibility graph of licenses, we identified 16 queries whose result set cannot be licensed. Table 9 shows these queries, their conflicting capable data sources and conflicting licenses. 10 queries need to be relaxed, they are shown in bold. We recall that the DBpedia license (CC BY-SA) is not compliant with the licenses of Jamendo (CC BY-NC-SA), Linked TCGA and Drug bank (CC BY-NC). The average time to check license conflicts is 296 milliseconds which is negligible.

Evaluation of Queries that Do Not Need Relaxation. Figure 8 presents the execution time of the 22 queries of LargeRDFBench that do not need relaxation. We identify two sets of queries.

---

[18] https://github.com/dice-group/CostFed.
[19] https://github.com/benjimor/FLiQuE.

- For 16 queries, {S2, S3, S4, S5, S7, S11, S12, S13, S14, C1, C2, C4, C6, C7, L2, L4}, FLiQue finds a license that can protect the result set when the query is executed on the complete federation. For these queries, the overhead of FLiQue is negligible and corresponds to the time to check license conflicts among the capable datasets. This overhead depends on the number of distinct licenses that protect the capable datasets.
- For 6 queries, {S1, S6, S9, C3, L1, L3}, FLiQue does not find a license that can protect the result set when the query is executed over the complete federation. However, it finds a sub-federation such that the original query returns a non-empty result set that is licensable. In this case, the overhead of FLiQue corresponds to the time to check license conflicts, to compute sub-federations, and to execute the original query on these sub-federations until the first result is returned. This overhead depends on the number of tested sub-federations. The number of sub-federations depends on the number of distinct conflicting licenses by query. In our test environment, this number is always 2. For instance, conflicting licenses CC BY-SA, CC BY-NC, and CC BY-NC-SA can be separated into two non-conflicting sets {CC BY-SA} and {CC BY-NC, and CC BY-NC-SA}. These sub-federations are ordered by the number of datasets in the federation. In the benchmark, the average time to generate the sub-federations and find a non-empty result set is 11020 milliseconds. For these 6 queries, we remark that this overhead is almost constant. That is because, a non-empty result set is found when FLiQue executes the original query on the second sub-federation.

Evaluation of Queries that Are Relaxed. Figure 9 presents the execution of the 10 queries of LargeRDFBench that need relaxation to return a non-empty result set that can be protected by a license. For each query, we compare the time to get the first result of the original query for CostFed, and the time to get the first result of the first candidate query found by FLiQue.

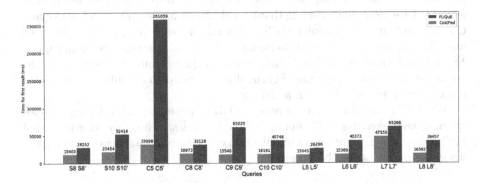

Fig. 9. Average time to get the first result of the 10 queries of LargeRDFBench that need relaxation to produce a licensable result set.

The FLiQue overhead corresponds to the time to check license conflicts to compute sub-federations, and to find the first candidate query.

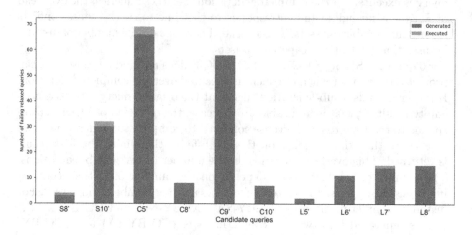

Fig. 10. Number of generated and executed failing relaxed queries until finding each candidate query.

We remark that the execution time of an original query and a candidate query is not comparable. They are not the same query, and they are not executed on the same number of data sources. The candidate queries are more general. To have an idea (non-representative) of the similarities, the maximum is 0.811 (L5'), the minimum is 0.077 (C8'), the average is 0.487, and the median is 0.603. Candidate queries and their similarities are included in Annex A.

Overhead varies a lot depending on the queries. It depends on the number of generated and executed failing relaxed queries, before finding the first candidate query. Figure 10 shows the number of failing relaxed queries, (1) generated, and (2) executed before finding each candidate query. Most of the relaxed queries generated are identified as failing thanks to data summaries. The candidate query $C5'$, is found after generating 69 failing relaxed queries, but only 3 were executed until finding the first one with non-empty result. In contrast, candidate query $S8'$ is found after generating 3 failing relaxed queries but executing only one. For 6 out of 10 relaxed queries, FLiQue does not need to execute any generated relaxed query to identify them as failing.

With this benchmark, on average FLiQue generates 21.4 failing relaxed queries, and executes 1.75 failing relaxed queries. Thus, we consider that FLiQue succeeds in limiting communication costs during the relaxation of queries whose result set cannot be licensed.

4.3 Discussion

[8,15] used in their experiments the datasets generated with the LUBM benchmark [11]. LUBM generates synthetic data as one data source and was developed

to evaluate systems with different reasoning capabilities. [15] used 7 queries with a number of triple patterns ranging from 2 to 5. [8] modified these 7 queries to added constraints. In their modified queries, triple patterns range from 2 to 15, the average is 7. Their experimental goal was to show the number of relaxed queries executed until obtaining top-k results.

Our goal is different. We aim to show that preserving licenses during federated query processing is possible. LargeRDFBench is the only benchmark with federated queries. It is composed of several real-world interlinked datasets whose federated queries were designed by domain specialists. This benchmark was not defined for reasoning. As it does not include ontologies[20] we searched them[21]. Several properties or classes of some datasets are not defined in the found ontologies, and hierarchies in concept ontologies are frequently undefined.

As LargeRDFBench was defined to evaluate federated query processing, its federated queries have many variables. Very few triple patterns have classes in objects or subjects. That is why query relaxation was mainly based on property relaxation. Only two classes in objects were relaxed (dbo:Drug in S10 and dbpedia:Drug in C9).

LargeRDFBench datasets are of multiple domains. They were chosen because they are interlinked, i.e., they have *owl:sameAs* relationships, the subject/object of one dataset exists in another dataset, or some predicates (like *title* and *genericName*) have the same literal values. The choice of these datasets was not focused on common classes or predicates, but on instances. That is why almost all relaxations ended in simple relaxations (except for L5 and L8 where *foaf:name* was relaxed to *rdfs:label*).

Although LargeRDFBench is not the ideal benchmark for evaluating FLiQue, we were able to demonstrate that federated query processing can ensure license compliance using query relaxation.

5   Conclusion and Perspectives

In this work, we propose FLiQue, a federated license-aware query processing strategy that guarantees that a license protects the result set of a federated SPARQL query. FLiQue is designed to detect and prevent license conflicts and gives informed feedback with licenses able to protect a result set of a federated query. If necessary, it applies distributed query relaxation to propose a set of most similar relaxed federated queries whose result set can be licensed. To our knowledge, this is the first work that uses query relaxation in a distributed environment. Our implementation extends an existing federated query engine with our license-aware query processing strategy. Our prototype demonstrates the feasibility of our approach. Experimental evaluation shows that FLiQue ensures license compliance with a limited overhead in terms of execution time. FLiQue is

---

[20] https://github.com/dice-group/LargeRDFBench.

[21] This is a compilation of all ontologies we found for LargeRDFFech datasets: https://raw.githubusercontent.com/benj-moreau/FLiQue/master/flique/ontologies/ontology.n3.

a step towards facilitating and encouraging the publication and reuse of licensed resources in the Web of Data. FLiQue is not a data access control strategy. Instead, it empowers well-intentioned data users in respecting the licenses of datasets involved in a federated query.

This work has several perspectives. One perspective considers other aspects of licenses related to usage contexts like jurisdiction, dates of reuse, etc. Another perspective is about estimating the selectivity of relaxed queries and use it to help users choose the best-relaxed query for their purposes. Information content measures are currently used to define similarity between queries; nevertheless, semantic similarity may also be used, for instance, *owl:sameAs* relationships.

A perspective not directly related to FLiQue but to the used benchmark, is to analyze the ontologies of datasets composing LargeRDFBench and complete them. Furthermore, it will be interesting to modify the federated queries to include more classes in subjects and objects.

A   Supplemental material

Listing 1.2. Query S8 followed by the candidate query S8'.

```
1  PREFIX drugbank: <http://www4.wiwiss.fu−berlin.de/drugbank/resource
       /drugbank/>
2  PREFIX dbo: <http://dbpedia.org/ontology/>
3
4  SELECT ?drug ?melt WHERE {
5    { ?drug drugbank:meltingPoint ?melt. }
6    UNION
7    { ?drug dbo:meltingPoint ?melt . }
8  }
9
10
11 SELECT ?drug ?melt WHERE {
12   { ?drug drugbank:meltingPoint ?melt. }
13   UNION
14   { ?drug ?1HmoLC ?melt . }
15 }
16
17 # Similarity: 0.666666666666666
```

Listing 1.3. Query S10 followed by the candidate query S10'.

```
1  PREFIX drugbank: <http://www4.wiwiss.fu−berlin.de/drugbank/resource
       /drugbank/>
2  PREFIX owl: <http://www.w3.org/2002/07/owl#>
3  PREFIX dbo: <http://dbpedia.org/ontology/>
4
5  SELECT ?Drug ?IntDrug ?IntEffect WHERE {
6    ?Drug a dbo:Drug .
7    ?y owl:sameAs ?Drug .
8    ?Int drugbank:interactionDrug1 ?y .
9    ?Int drugbank:interactionDrug2 ?IntDrug .
10   ?Int drugbank:text ?IntEffect .
11 }
12
13
14 SELECT ?Drug ?IntDrug ?IntEffect WHERE {
15   ?Drug ?zkB8o2 ?OKS9kY .
16   ?y ?Y2df3t ?Drug .
```

```
17    ?Int drugbank:interactionDrug1 ?y .
18    ?Int ?Q6kLIS ?IntDrug .
19    ?Int drugbank:text ?IntEffect .
20 }
21
22 # Similarity: 0.11111111111
```

Listing 1.4. Query C5 followed by the candidate query C5'.

```
1  PREFIX linkedmdb: <http://data.linkedmdb.org/resource/movie/>
2  PREFIX dcterms: <http://purl.org/dc/terms/>
3  PREFIX dbpedia: <http://dbpedia.org/ontology/>
4  PREFIX rdfs: <http://www.w3.org/2000/01/rdf-schema#>
5
6  SELECT ?actor ?movie ?movieTitle ?movieDate ?birthDate ?spouseName
7  {
8    ?actor rdfs:label ?actor_name_en .
9    ?actor dbpedia:birthDate ?birthDate .
10   ?actor dbpedia:spouse ?spouseURI .
11   ?spouseURI rdfs:label ?spouseName .
12   ?imdbactor linkedmdb:actor_name ?actor_name.
13   ?movie linkedmdb:actor ?imdbactor .
14   ?movie dcterms:title ?movieTitle .
15   ?movie dcterms:date ?movieDate .
16   FILTER(STR(?actor_name_en ) = STR(?actor_name))
17 }
18
19 SELECT ?actor ?movie ?movieTitle ?movieDate ?birthDate ?spouseName
20 {
21   ?actor rdfs:label ?actor_name_en .
22   ?actor ?SxzR4W ?birthDate .
23   ?actor ?1OCiE4 ?spouseURI .
24   ?spouseURI rdfs:label ?spouseName .
25   ?imdbactor linkedmdb:actor_name ?actor_name .
26   ?movie linkedmdb:actor ?imdbactor .
27   ?movie dcterms:title ?movieTitle .
28   ?movie dcterms:date ?movieDate .
29   FILTER(STR(?actor_name_en ) = STR(?actor_name))
30 }
31 # Similarity: 0.44444444444
```

Listing 1.5. Query C8 followed by the candidate query C8'.

```
1  PREFIX swc: <http://data.semanticweb.org/ns/swc/ontology#>
2  PREFIX swrc: <http://swrc.ontoware.org/ontology#>
3  PREFIX eswc: <http://data.semanticweb.org/conference/eswc/>
4  PREFIX iswc: <http://data.semanticweb.org/conference/iswc/2009/>
5  PREFIX foaf: <http://xmlns.com/foaf/0.1/>
6  PREFIX purl: <http://purl.org/ontology/bibo/>
7  PREFIX dbpedia: <http://dbpedia.org/ontology/>
8  PREFIX rdfs: <http://www.w3.org/2000/01/rdf-schema#>
9
10 SELECT DISTINCT * WHERE
11 {
12   ?paper swc:isPartOf iswc:proceedings .
13   iswc:proceedings swrc:address ?proceedingAddress.
14   ?paper swrc:author ?author .
15   ?author swrc:affiliation ?affiliation ;
16   ?author rdfs:label ?fullnames ;
17   ?author foaf:based_near ?place.
18   ?place dbpedia:capital ?capital .
19   ?place dbpedia:populationDensity ?populationDensity .
20   ?place dbpedia:governmentType ?governmentType .
21   ?place dbpedia:language ?language .
22   ?place dbpedia:leaderTitle ?leaderTitle .
23 }
```

```
24
25
26  SELECT DISTINCT * WHERE
27  {
28    ?paper swc:isPartOf iswc:proceedings .
29    iswc:proceedings swrc:address ?proceedingAddress.
30    ?paper swrc:author ?author .
31    ?author swrc:affiliation ?affiliation .
32    ?author rdfs:label ?fullnames .
33    ?author foaf:based_near ?place.
34    ?place ?mM9RIT ?capital .
35    ?place ?cZP8iP ?populationDensity .
36    ?place ?Pp7c1t ?governmentType .
37    ?place ?z2uYJB ?language .
38    ?place ?de7OQZ ?leaderTitle .
39  }
40
41  # Similarity: 0.07777777777
```

Listing 1.6. Query C9 followed by the candidate query C9'.

```
1   PREFIX dbpedia: <http://dbpedia.org/ontology/>
2   PREFIX rdf: <http://www.w3.org/1999/02/22-rdf-syntax-ns#>
3   PREFIX owl: <http://www.w3.org/2002/07/owl#>
4   PREFIX drugbank: <http://www4.wiwiss.fu-berlin.de/drugbank/resource
        /drugbank/>
5
6   SELECT * WHERE
7   {
8     ?Drug rdf:type dbpedia:Drug .
9     ?drugbankDrug owl:sameAs ?Drug .
10    ?InteractionName drugbank:interactionDrug1 ?drugbankDrug .
11    ?InteractionName drugbank:interactionDrug2 ?drugbankDrug2 .
12    ?InteractionName drugbank:text ?IntEffect .
13    OPTIONAL
14    {
15      ?drugbankDrug drugbank:affectedOrganism 'Humans and other
            mammals' .
16      ?drugbankDrug drugbank:description ?description .
17      ?drugbankDrug drugbank:structure ?structure .
18      ?drugbankDrug drugbank:casRegistryNumber ?casRegistryNumber .
19    }
20  }
21  ORDER BY (?drugbankDrug)
22
23
24  SELECT * WHERE
25  {
26    ?Drug ?0OgzMk ?Cvqg5H .
27    ?drugbankDrug ?c5DqMr ?Drug .
28    ?InteractionName drugbank:interactionDrug1 ?drugbankDrug .
29    ?InteractionName drugbank:interactionDrug2 ?drugbankDrug2 .
30    ?InteractionName drugbank:text ?IntEffect .
31    OPTIONAL
32    {
33      ?drugbankDrug drugbank:affectedOrganism 'Humans and other
            mammals' .
34      drugbank:description ?description .
35      drugbank:structure ?structure .
36      drugbank:casRegistryNumber ?casRegistryNumber .
37    }
38  }
39  ORDER BY (?drugbankDrug)
40
41  # Similarity: 0.222222222222
```

Listing 1.7. Query C10 followed by the candidate query C10'.

```
1   PREFIX tcga: <http://tcga.deri.ie/schema/>
2   PREFIX kegg: <http://bio2rdf.org/ns/kegg#>
3   PREFIX dbpedia: <http://dbpedia.org/ontology/>
4   PREFIX drugbank: <http://www4.wiwiss.fu-berlin.de/drugbank/resource
        /drugbank/>
5   PREFIX purl: <http://purl.org/dc/terms/>
6
7   SELECT  DISTINCT ?patient  ?gender ?country ?popDensity ?drugName ?
        indication ?formula ?compound
8   WHERE
9   {
10    ?uri tcga:bcr_patient_barcode ?patient .
11    ?patient tcga:gender ?gender .
12    ?patient dbpedia:country ?country .
13    ?country dbpedia:populationDensity ?popDensity.
14    ?patient tcga:bcr_drug_barcode ?drugbcr.
15    ?drugbcr tcga:drug_name ?drugName.
16    ?drgBnkDrg drugbank:genericName ?drugName.
17    ?drgBnkDrg drugbank:indication ?indication.
18    ?drgBnkDrg drugbank:chemicalFormula ?formula.
19    ?drgBnkDrg drugbank:keggCompoundId ?compound .
20  }
21
22
23  SELECT  DISTINCT ?patient  ?gender ?country ?popDensity ?drugName ?
        indication ?formula ?compound
24  WHERE
25  {
26    ?uri tcga:bcr_patient_barcode ?patient .
27    ?patient tcga:gender ?gender.
28    ?patient dbpedia:country ?country.
29    ?country ?7sqC60 ?popDensity.
30    ?patient tcga:bcr_drug_barcode ?drugbcr.
31    ?drugbcr tcga:drug_name ?drugName.
32    ?drgBnkDrg drugbank:genericName ?drugName.
33    ?drgBnkDrg drugbank:indication ?indication.
34    ?drgBnkDrg drugbank:chemicalFormula ?formula.
35    ?drgBnkDrg drugbank:keggCompoundId ?compound .
36  }
37
38  # Similarity: 0.66666666666
```

Listing 1.8. Query L5 followed by the candidate query L5'.

```
1   PREFIX dbpedia: <http://dbpedia.org/resource/>
2   PREFIX dbprop: <http://dbpedia.org/property/>
3   PREFIX dbowl: <http://dbpedia.org/ontology/>
4   PREFIX foaf: <http://xmlns.com/foaf/0.1/>
5   PREFIX owl: <http://www.w3.org/2002/07/owl#>
6   PREFIX rdf: <http://www.w3.org/1999/02/22-rdf-syntax-ns#>
7   PREFIX rdfs: <http://www.w3.org/2000/01/rdf-schema#>
8   PREFIX skos: <http://www.w3.org/2004/02/skos/core#>
9   PREFIX factbook: <http://www4.wiwiss.fu-berlin.de/factbook/ns#>
10  PREFIX mo: <http://purl.org/ontology/mo/>
11  PREFIX dc: <http://purl.org/dc/elements/1.1/>
12  PREFIX fb: <http://rdf.freebase.com/ns/>
13
14  SELECT * WHERE {
15    ?a dbowl:artist dbpedia:Michael_Jackson .
16    ?a rdf:type dbowl:Album .
17    ?a foaf:name ?n .
18  }
19
20
21  SELECT * WHERE {
```

```
22    ?a dbowl:artist dbpedia:Michael_Jackson .
23    ?a rdf:type dbowl:Album .
24    ?a rdfs:label ?n .
25  }
26
27  # Similarity:  0.8115399282213058
```

Listing 1.9. Query L6 followed by the candidate query L6'.

```
1   PREFIX dbpedia: <http://dbpedia.org/resource/>
2   PREFIX dbowl: <http://dbpedia.org/ontology/>
3   PREFIX owl: <http://www.w3.org/2002/07/owl#>
4   PREFIX linkedMDB: <http://data.linkedmdb.org/resource/>
5   PREFIX foaf: <http://xmlns.com/foaf/0.1/>
6   PREFIX geo: <http://www.geonames.org/ontology#>
7
8   SELECT * WHERE {
9    ?director dbowl:nationality dbpedia:Italy .
10   ?film dbowl:director ?director.
11   ?x owl:sameAs ?film .
12   ?x foaf:based_near ?y .
13   ?y geo:officialName ?n .
14  }
15
16
17  SELECT * WHERE {
18   ?director dbowl:nationality dbpedia:Italy .
19   ?film dbowl:director ?director.
20   ?x owl:sameAs ?film .
21   ?x ?6GKJwd ?y .
22   ?y geo:officialName ?n .
23  }
24
25  # Similarity:  0.66666666666
```

Listing 1.10. Query L7 followed by the candidate query L7'.

```
1   PREFIX tcga: <http://tcga.deri.ie/schema/>
2   PREFIX dbpedia: <http://dbpedia.org/ontology/>
3   SELECT DISTINCT ?patient ?p ?o
4   WHERE
5   {
6    ?uri tcga:bcr_patient_barcode ?patient .
7    ?patient dbpedia:country ?country.
8    ?country dbpedia:populationDensity ?popDensity.
9    ?patient tcga:bcr_aliquot_barcode ?aliquot.
10   ?aliquot ?p ?o.
11  }
12
13
14  SELECT DISTINCT ?patient ?p ?o
15  WHERE
16  {
17   ?uri tcga:bcr_patient_barcode ?patient .
18   ?patient dbpedia:country ?country .
19   ?country ?cG4icP ?popDensity.
20   ?patient tcga:bcr_aliquot_barcode ?aliquot .
21   ?aliquot ?p ?o .
22  }
23
24  # Similarity:  0.66666666666
```

Listing 1.11. Query L8 followed by the candidate query L8'.

```
1   PREFIX kegg: <http://bio2rdf.org/ns/kegg#>
2   PREFIX drugbank: <http://www4.wiwiss.fu-berlin.de/drugbank/resource
       /drugbank/>
3   PREFIX owl: <http://www.w3.org/2002/07/owl#>
4   PREFIX foaf: <http://xmlns.com/foaf/0.1/>
5   PREFIX skos: <http://www.w3.org/2004/02/skos/core#>
6
7   SELECT * WHERE {
8     ?drug drugbank:drugCategory drugbank:micronutrient .
9     ?drug drugbank:casRegistryNumber ?id .
10    ?drug owl:sameAs ?s .
11    ?s foaf:name ?o .
12    ?s skos:subject ?sub .
13  }
14
15
16  SELECT * WHERE {
17    ?drug drugbank:drugCategory drugbank:micronutrient .
18    ?drug drugbank:casRegistryNumber ?id .
19    ?drug ?XKeC36 ?s .
20    ?s rdfs:label ?o .
21    ?s skos:subject ?sub .
22  }
23
24  # Similarity: 0.5410266188142039
```

References

1. Bizer, C., Heath, T., Berners-Lee, T.: Linked data: the story so far. In: Semantic Services, Interoperability and Web Applications: Emerging Concepts. IGI Global (2011)
2. Bonatti, P.A., Decker, S., Polleres, A., Presutti, V.: Knowledge graphs: new directions for knowledge representation on the semantic web (gagstuhl seminar 18371). Dagstuhl reports (2019)
3. Cabrio, E., Palmero Aprosio, A., Villata, S.: These are your rights. In: Presutti, V., d'Amato, C., Gandon, F., d'Aquin, M., Staab, S., Tordai, A. (eds.) ESWC 2014. LNCS, vol. 8465, pp. 255–269. Springer, Cham (2014). https://doi.org/10.1007/978-3-319-07443-6_18
4. Čebirić, Š, et al.: Summarizing semantic graphs: a survey. VLDB J. **28**(3), 295–327 (2018). https://doi.org/10.1007/s00778-018-0528-3
5. Costabello, L., Villata, S., Gandon, F.: Context-aware access control for RDF graph stores. In: European Conference on Artificial Intelligence (ECAI) (2012)
6. Cyganiak, R., Hausenblas, M.: Describing linked datasets - on the design and usage of voiD, the "vocabulary of interlinked datasets". In: Linked Data on the Web Workshop (LDOW) (2009)
7. Ferré, S.: Answers partitioning and lazy joins for efficient query relaxation and application to similarity search. In: Gangemi, A., et al. (eds.) ESWC 2018. LNCS, vol. 10843, pp. 209–224. Springer, Cham (2018). https://doi.org/10.1007/978-3-319-93417-4_14
8. Fokou, G., Jean, S., Hadjali, A., Baron, M.: RDF query relaxation strategies based on failure causes. In: Sack, H., Blomqvist, E., d'Aquin, M., Ghidini, C., Ponzetto, S.P., Lange, C. (eds.) ESWC 2016. LNCS, vol. 9678, pp. 439–454. Springer, Cham (2016). https://doi.org/10.1007/978-3-319-34129-3_27

9. Gabillon, A., Letouzey, L.: A view based access control model for SPARQL. In: International Conference on Network and System Security (NSS) (2010)
10. Görlitz, O., Staab, S.: SPLENDID: SPARQL endpoint federation exploiting VOID descriptions. In: Workshop Consuming Linked Data (COLD) Collocated with ISWC (2011)
11. Guo, Y., Pan, Z., Heflin, J.: LUBM: a benchmark for OWL knowledge base systems. J. Web Semant. **3**(2–3), 158–182 (2005)
12. Hartig, O., Vidal, M.E., Freytag, J.C.: Federated semantic data management (dagstuhl seminar 17262). Dagstuhl reports (2017)
13. Havur, G., et al.: DALICC: a framework for publishing and consuming data assets legally. In: International Conference on Semantic Systems (SEMANTICS), Poster&Demo (2018)
14. Hogan, A., et al.: Knowledge graphs. CoRR abs/2003.02320 (2020)
15. Huang, H., Liu, C., Zhou, X.: Approximating query answering on RDF databases. J. World Wide Web **15**, 89–114 (2012). https://doi.org/10.1007/s11280-011-0131-7
16. Hurtado, C.A., Poulovassilis, A., Wood, P.T.: Query relaxation in RDF. In: Spaccapietra, S. (ed.) Journal on Data Semantics X. LNCS, vol. 4900, pp. 31–61. Springer, Heidelberg (2008). https://doi.org/10.1007/978-3-540-77688-8_2
17. Iannella, R., Villata, S.: ODRL information model 2.2. W3C Recommendation (2018)
18. Kapitsaki, G.M., Kramer, F., Tselikas, N.D.: Automating the license compatibility process in open source software with SPDX. J. Syst. Softw. **131**, 386–401 (2017)
19. Khan, Y., et al.: SAFE: policy aware SPARQL query federation over RDF data cubes. In: Semantic Web Applications and Tools for Life Sciences (SWAT4LS) (2014)
20. Kirrane, S., Abdelrahman, A., Mileo, A., Decker, S.: Secure manipulation of linked data. In: Alani, H., et al. (eds.) ISWC 2013. LNCS, vol. 8218, pp. 248–263. Springer, Heidelberg (2013). https://doi.org/10.1007/978-3-642-41335-3_16
21. Moreau, B., Serrano-Alvarado, P., Perrin, M., Desmontils, E.: A license-based search engine. In: Hitzler, P., et al. (eds.) ESWC 2019. LNCS, vol. 11762, pp. 130–135. Springer, Cham (2019). https://doi.org/10.1007/978-3-030-32327-1_26
22. Moreau, B., Serrano-Alvarado, P., Perrin, M., Desmontils, E.: Modelling the compatibility of licenses. In: Hitzler, P., et al. (eds.) ESWC 2019. LNCS, vol. 11503, pp. 255–269. Springer, Cham (2019). https://doi.org/10.1007/978-3-030-21348-0_17
23. Oguz, D., Ergenc, B., Yin, S., Dikenelli, O., Hameurlain, A.: Federated query processing on linked data: a qualitative survey and open challenges. Knowl. Eng. Rev. **30**(5), 545–563 (2015)
24. Oulmakhzoune, S., Cuppens-Boulahia, N., Cuppens, F., Morucci, S., Barhamgi, M., Benslimane, D.: Privacy query rewriting algorithm instrumented by a privacy-aware access control model. Ann. Telecommun. **69**, 3–19 (2014). https://doi.org/10.1007/s12243-013-0365-8
25. Pellegrini, T., et al.: DALICC: a license management framework for digital assets. In: Proceedings of the Internationales Rechtsinformatik Symposion (IRIS), p. 10 (2019)
26. Qudus, U., Saleem, M., Ngonga Ngomo, A.C., Lee, Y.K.: An empirical evaluation of cost-based federated SPARQL query processing engines. CoRR, **abs/2104.00984** (2021). https://arxiv.org/abs/2104.00984

27. Quilitz, B., Leser, U.: Querying distributed RDF data sources with SPARQL. In: Bechhofer, S., Hauswirth, M., Hoffmann, J., Koubarakis, M. (eds.) ESWC 2008. LNCS, vol. 5021, pp. 524–538. Springer, Heidelberg (2008). https://doi.org/10.1007/978-3-540-68234-9_39

28. Reddivari, P., Finin, T., Joshi, A., et al.: Policy-based access control for an RDF store. In: Workshop Semantic Web for Collaborative Knowledge Acquisition (SWeCKa) Collocated with IJCAI (2007)

29. Resnik, P.: Using information content to evaluate semantic similarity in a taxonomy. In: International Joint Conference on Artificial Intelligence (IJCAI) (1995)

30. Rodríguez Doncel, V., Gómez-Pérez, A., Villata, S.: A dataset of RDF licenses. In: Legal Knowledge and Information Systems Conference (ICLKIS) (2014)

31. Sadeh, N., Acquisti, A., Breaux, T.D., Cranor, L.F., et al.: Towards usable privacy policies: semi-automatically extracting data practices from websites' privacy policies. In: Symposium on Usable Privacy and Security (SOUPS) (2014). Poster

32. Saleem, M., Hasnain, A., Ngomo, A.C.N.: LargeRDFBench: a billion triples benchmark for SPARQL endpoint federation. J. Semant. Web **48**, 85–125 (2018)

33. Saleem, M., Ngonga Ngomo, A.-C.: HiBISCuS: hypergraph-based source selection for SPARQL endpoint federation. In: Presutti, V., d'Amato, C., Gandon, F., d'Aquin, M., Staab, S., Tordai, A. (eds.) ESWC 2014. LNCS, vol. 8465, pp. 176–191. Springer, Cham (2014). https://doi.org/10.1007/978-3-319-07443-6_13

34. Saleem, M., Potocki, A., Soru, T., Hartig, O., Ngomo, A.N.: CostFed: cost-based query optimization for SPARQL endpoint federation. In: International Conference on Semantic Systems (SEMANTICS) (2018)

35. Schwarte, A., Haase, P., Hose, K., Schenkel, R., Schmidt, M.: FedX: optimization techniques for federated query processing on linked data. In: Aroyo, L., et al. (eds.) ISWC 2011. LNCS, vol. 7031, pp. 601–616. Springer, Heidelberg (2011). https://doi.org/10.1007/978-3-642-25073-6_38

36. Seneviratne, O., Kagal, L., Berners-Lee, T.: Policy-aware content reuse on the web. In: Bernstein, A., et al. (eds.) ISWC 2009. LNCS, vol. 5823, pp. 553–568. Springer, Heidelberg (2009). https://doi.org/10.1007/978-3-642-04930-9_35

37. Villata, S., Gandon, F.: Licenses compatibility and composition in the web of data. In: Workshop Consuming Linked Data (COLD) Collocated with ISWC (2012)

38. Wheeler, D.A.: The Free-Libre/Open Source Software (FLOSS) License Slide (2017). https://www.dwheeler.com/essays/floss-license-slide.pdf

Author Index

Printed in the United States
by Baker & Taylor Publisher Services